ANGEL

From KETTI FRINGS'
Pulitzer Prize Winning Play
*"*LOOK HOMEWARD ANGEL*"*
derived from the THOMAS WOLFE *novel*

Libretto by KETTI FRINGS & PETER UDELL

Lyrics by PETER UDELL

Music by GARY GELD

SAMUEL FRENCH, INC.
25 WEST 45TH STREET   NEW YORK 10036
7623 SUNSET BOULEVARD   HOLLYWOOD 90046
LONDON   *TORONTO*

ANGEL opened at the Minskoff Theatre, May 10, 1978, under the direction of Philip Rose. Choreography was by Robert Tucker; Scenery by Ming Cho Lee; Lighting by John Gleason; Costumes by Perl Somner; Orchestrations by Don Walker; Musical Direction and Dance Arrangements by William Cox; The Production Stage Manager was Steve Zweigbaum.

CAST

(in order of appearance)

HELEN GANT	*Donna Davis*
BEN GANT	*Joel Higgins*
MRS. FATTY PERT	*Patti Allison*
MRS. SNOWDEN	*Grace Carney*
EUGENE GANT	*Don Scardino*
ELIZA GANT	*Frances Sternhagen*
WILL PENTLAND	*Elek Hartman*
FLORRY MANGLE	*Rebecca Seay*
MRS. CLATT	*Justine Johnston*
JAKE CLATT	*Gene Masoner*
MR. FARREL	*Billy Beckham*
MISS BROWN	*Jayne Barnett*
LAURA JAMES	*Leslie Ann Ray*
W.O. GANT	*Fred Gwynne*
DR. MAGUIRE	*Daniel Keyes*
JOE TARKINGTON	*Rex David Hays*
REED MCKINNEY	*Carl Nicholas*
TIM LAUGHRAN	*Norman Stotz*
MADAME VICTORIA	*Patricia Englund*

3

MUSICAL NUMBERS

ACT ONE

ANGEL THEME .... *Orchestra*

ALL THE COMFORTS OF HOME .... *Boarders*

LIKE THE EAGLES FLY .... *Ben Gant*

MAKE A LITTLE SUNSHINE .. *Eliza Gant, Eugene Gant,
Ben Gant*

FINGERS AND TOES ...... *W. O. Gant, Tim Laughran,
Reed McKinney, Joe Tarkington*

FATTY .... *Ben Gant*

ASTORIA GLORIA .... *Fatty Pert and Boarders*

RAILBIRD .... *Eugene Gant*

IF I EVER LOVED HIM .... *Laura James*

A DIME AIN'T WORTH A NICKEL .... *Ben Gant,
Fatty Pert*

I GOT A DREAM TO SLEEP ON .... *Eugene Gant*

DRIFTING .... *Eliza Gant*

ACT TWO

I CAN'T BELIEVE IT'S YOU .... *W. O. Gant,
Madame Victoria*

FEELIN' LOVED .... *Eugene Gant, Laura James*

A MEDLEY .... *Ben Gant, Fatty Pert,
Eliza Gant, Laura James*

TOMORROW I'M GONNA BE OLD .... *W. O. Gant*

FEELIN' LOVED (Reprise) .. *Eugene Gant, Laura James*

HOW DO YOU SAY GOODBYE .... *Laura James*

GANT'S WALTZ .... *W. O. Gant, Eliza Gant*

LIKE THE EAGLES FLY (Reprise) ...... *Eugene Gant*

5

Angel

ACT ONE

OVERTURE: *ANGEL THEME*

SCENE 1

*The Dixieland Boarding House, Altamont, North Carolina.
An early autumn afternoon, 1916. The house is a two
story frame structure with a rambling, unplanned gabular
appearance. Most of the furniture is badly worn and out
of style. On the typically Southern veranda which embraces the front and one side of the house are shabby
pieces of wicker; a chair by the front door; to its Right
a small table, a bench, and a rocker at the far Right end
of the unit. There is a sign above the front door, electri-
cally lighted at night: DIXIELAND. Behind the front
door, a center hall; to its Right a parlor with piano, couch
and side screen door entrance to the veranda. The dining
room with sideboard, telephone, tables and chairs is Left
of the hallway. The kitchen, Right, and hidden from view,
and back door, Left, complete this section of the house.
Directly above the parlor area, to the Right, is the entrance to the keeping room and staircase to the second
floor landing. To the Right of the landing, a door presum-
ably leading to other areas of the house. To the Left, a
room to let. To the Left of the house, a tree swing and
lawn furniture complete the area.*

*As the curtain rises the BOARDERS are discovered in various
areas of the house. They are:* JAKE CLATT, *30, an insensi-
tive boor.* MRS. CLATT, *60,* JAKE'S *mother with a coarse
smile and dyed hair.* FLORRY MANGLE, *20, wistful, humor-
less, interested in* JAKE. MRS. SNOWDEN, *50, quiet, un-
obtrusive, lonely.* MISS BROWN, *36, prim on the surface,
but with the marks of the amateur prostitute.* MR. FARREL,
*60, a piano teacher, new to Dixieland. They begin sing-
ing posed in the style of the period.*

7

SONG: *"ALL THE COMFORTS OF HOME"*

BOARDERS.
A FRIENDLY SMILE IN THE MORNIN'
A PRIVATE ROOM OF YOUR OWN
A WINDOW, A SHOWER
A POT WITH A FLOWER
ALL THE COMFORTS OF HOME
MR. FARREL.
A FINE OL' UPRIGHT PIANA
MISS BROWN.
WITH JUST THE HAPPIEST TONE
MR. FARREL.
UNBUTTON MY COLLAR
MISS BROWN.
WE'LL SING IN THE PARLOR
BOARDERS.
ALL THE COMFORTS OF HOME

A FAM'LY YOU CAN RELY ON
DEVOTED ONLY TO YOU
MRS. PERT.
A READY SHOULDER TO CRY ON
BOARDERS.
IF EVER YOU FEEL SAD AND BLUE
MRS. CLATT.
THE DAILY PAPER'S DELIVERED
MR. FARREL.
AND IN THE FOYER, 'S A PHONE
MISS MANGLE, MRS. PERT, MRS. SNOWDEN.
CONVEN'ENCE AND STATUS
THE PERFECT HIATUS
BOARDERS.
ALL THE COMFORTS OF HOME, TO COMFORT
    YOU
ALL THE COMFORTS OF HOME
MISS MANGLE.
THE TUB IS GENUINE PORCELAIN
MRS. PERT.
THE FAUCET HANDLES ARE CHROME

Mrs. Clatt.
THE TONIC AND TALCUM
    IS SURELY A W'LCOME
Boarders.
ALL THE COMFORTS OF HOME

A ROCKER ON THE VERANDA
THE PERFECT NOOK FOR A CHAT
A VIEW THAT COULDN'T BE GRANDA'
THERE'S EVEN A HOOK FOR YOUR HAT
Joe.
UNPACK MY SOCKS AND MY GARTERS
Jake.
SET OUT MY TOOTHBRUSH AND COMB
Mrs. Pert, Mrs. Clatt.
IT'S ALL SO APPEALIN'
    THAT WONDERFUL FEELIN'
Boarders.
ALL THE COMFORTS OF HOME, TO COMFORT
    YOU
ALL THE COMFORTS OF HOME
ALL THE COMFORTS OF HOME.
HOME.

(Helen Gant *enters from the front door of the house. She is gaunt, raw-boned, in her middle twenties, often nervous, intense, irritable and abusive, though basically generous, the hysteria of excitement constantly lurking in her. It is a spiritual and physical necessity for her to exhaust herself in service to others, though her grievances, especially in the service to her mother, are many. She rings dinner bell.*)

Helen. Dinner! (*The* Boarders *enter the house complainin about the food and life style at the boarding house. They each take their particular place at the dinner table.*)
    Jake. Hope she doesn't serve yesterday's pop-overs.
    Mrs. Clatt. I suppose it will be watery soup again.
    Mrs. Snowden. Maybe once we'll have celery and olives. I just adore a relish plate . . . don't you?
    Mrs. Clatt. Yes I do, but how often do we get it? (Ben Gant *enter Left. He is sometimes scowling and surly, but he is the hero protector of those he loves, with quiet authority*

*and a passion for home which is fundamental. He crosses up
on the veranda, picks up a newspaper, and sits on the bench
as* HELEN *returns from the dining room.*)

HELEN. Ben, where's Mama?

BEN. How should I know?

HELEN. I'm gonna have to serve that entire dinner alone. I
believe she's just off somewhere with Uncle Will and I'm left
alone in the kitchen to slave for a bunch of old, cheap
boarders! And do I ever hear her say a word of thanks?

BOARDERS. (*From dining room.*) Helen, Helen . . .

HELEN. Help. Help. (HELEN *returns to serving the*
BOARDERS. MRS. PERT *enters the veranda from the side door.*
*"*FATTY*"* PERT *is a generous, somewhat boozy woman. She
sneaks up behind* BEN *and puts her hands over his eyes.*)

BEN. Mrs. Pert!

MRS. PERT. How did you guess?

BEN. I felt the vibrations.

MRS. PERT. Oh, Ben, I do declare you take advantage of my
good nature. (MRS. PERT *sits down alongside* BEN. *She sets
her knitting basket on the floor, takes out the wool, and
proceeds to knit. Pause.*)

BEN. I'm happy when I'm with you.

MRS. PERT. That's good, s'am I. I wish you'd known me
when I was younger, before my first husband.

BEN. You are young. (*Hugging her.*) I bet you weren't half
as nice and warm and round as you are now.

MRS. PERT. Ben, don't ever let your mother hear you say
things like that. What would she think?

BEN. Who cares what she thinks?

MRS. PERT. Honey. I only hope that when the right girl
comes along, you won't be sorry for the affection you've
lavished on me.

BEN. Fatty, I don't want the right girl. (*Smiles at her.
Resumes reading the paper.*) It says here there's an American
flying corps forming in Canada. (*Pause. Excited, he crosses
Left.*) Somebody's got to drive the Huns from the skies, Fatty.
Poor old England can't be expected to do it alone.

MRS. PERT. It's their mess, isn't it? Don't get so upset. Ben
honey, what are you thinking of?

BEN. All my life, Fatty, in this one burg, Fatty! It's like
being caught in a photograph and besides getting away, I'd
be doing my bit.

MRS. PERT. Would they take you so old?
BEN. This article says eighteen to thirty-two.
MRS. PERT. Aren't the physical standards pretty high?
BEN. Listen to her! I'm in good condition!
MRS. PERT. You're twenty pounds underweight! I never saw anybody like you for not eating.
BEN. Dr. Maguire gave me a thorough checkup just this spring.
MRS. PERT. How would your family feel if you went?
BEN. (*Takes her hand.*) What family? The batty boarders? Apologies, Fatty. You know I don't consider you one of them. Except for Gene, nobody'd even know I was gone. (*MUSIC CUE.*) Just think, Fatty . . . to fly up there and rush like the wind; a fella could spin like a pinwheel. Gant's comet, they'll call me. I'll write my name in the stars.

SONG: *"LIKE THE EAGLES FLY"*

I'M GONNA FLY LIKE THE EAGLES FLY
WAY UP HIGH
IN THE SKY
SEE ALL THE WORLD WITH AN EAGLE'S EYE
AND KNOW THAT I LIVED WHEN I DIE

I'M GONNA DRIFT ON A SUMMER BREEZE
'CROSS THE SEAS
AS I PLEASE
ONE THOUSAND MILES ABOVE THE TREES
AND BLESSED BE THE LORD WHEN I SNEEZE

CLIMBIN' AND DIVIN' AND CIRCLIN' AROUND
FREER THAN FREE I'LL BE WAY OFF THE
     GROUND
SWOOPIN' AND LOOPIN', THE HAPPIEST BIRD
RIDIN' THE CLOUDS LIKE SOME BUFFALO HERD

I'M GONNA SAIL LIKE THE EAGLES SAIL
FEATHERED TAIL
OUT OF JAIL
KISS ALL MY CARES AND MY WOES GOODBYE
     WITH SUN ON MY WINGS, I WILL FLY
FLY LIKE THE EAGLES FLY
WAY UP HIGH IN THE SKY.

MRS. PERT. Yes, you will. I'm sure you will.

BEN. I'm gonna do it.

MRS. SNOWDEN. (*Leaning out of front door.*) Mrs. Pert, they're just about to eat your charlotte russe. (*Exits.*)

MRS. PERT. I gave up the soup and the chicken, but I'm not giving up dessert . . . I'll see you a little later, Ben. (*Exits into house, leaving knitting. The House Unit revolves to POSITION #2 allowing more prominence to the Right area of the structure.* EUGENE's *head has appeared in window above.*)

EUGENE. My brother, the woman lover. They all seem to run from you and no wonder.

BEN. (*Looking up at window.*) Whatcha doin', kid?

EUGENE. Writin'.

BEN. Writin'? Better not let Mama catch you this time of day. What you writin' about?

EUGENE.
You. My brother Ben; His face is like a piece of slightly
yellow ivory. His mouth is like a knife
when he fastens his hard white fingers
and his scrawling eyes upon a thing
        he wants to fix
He sniffs with sharp and private concentration through his
        long, pointed nose. Thus women looking, feel a well of
        tenderness
For his pointed, bumpy always scowling face
(ELIZA's *voice is heard Offstage.*)

BEN. Watch out . . . here comes Mama. (EUGENE *disappears thru door at Right end of second floor landing.* BEN *crosses to the Right end of the veranda and resumes reading newspaper seated on rocker.* ELIZA *enters the yard from Left with* WILL PENTLAND, *her brother.* ELIZA GANT *is of Scotch descent, with all the acquisitiveness and fancied premonitions of the Scotch. She is mercurial, with dauntless energy, greed and love. She is carrying real estate circulars and two geranium filled flower pots.* WILL *is paunchy, successful, secure, a real estate broker. He carries grocery basket and one flower pot. They do not notice* BEN.)

ELIZA. Twenty thousand dollars! Oh, Will, I don't know if I can make him do it.

WILL. Well, you're gonna have to sit him down and make him listen to you.

ELIZA. Sit him down! That's a good one, that's a good one. I'll vow I never saw such a man. What little we have got, I've had to fight for tooth and nail, tooth and nail! Like the fellow says, there's no fool like an old fool! Of course Mr. Gant's been a fool all his life. Well, I'm going to get after him right today about that bank offer. (*She takes packages from* WILL *and exits to kitchen.*)

WILL. Let me know when you've warmed him up enough to talk to him.

ELIZA. (*Returning, takes pot from* WILL.) It'll take a good deal of warming up, I can tell you. He's so stubborn about that precious old marble yard.

WILL. Well, Sis, you had to have an artistic husband.

ELIZA. Artistic? If you call drinking and carousing artistic, he's a master all right. Why, the money that man squanders every year on liquor alone would buy all kinds of downtown property to say nothing of paying off this place. Thank heavens he's gotten too old to go to that *woman*, Madame Victoria's *house.* (*Sigh.*) We could be well-to-do people now if we'd started at the beginning.

WILL. Give me a jingle when you want me to talk to him. (WILL *exits Left.*)

ELIZA. Thanks, Will. I appreciate it. (ELIZA *locks real estate papers away in parlor desk.* BEN *coughs and* ELIZA *is aware that he has heard her previous conversation with* WILL.) Ben! What are you doing home at this hour! Shouldn't you be at the newspaper?

BEN. I'm working late afternoons this week.

ELIZA. Oh . . . will you get dinner downtown?

BEN. I usually do.

ELIZA. (*Crossing to him thru Right door.*) You always sound so short with me, Ben. Why is that? You don't even look at me. You know I can't stand not being looked at by the person I'm talking to. (*Touching his forehead.*) Don't you feel well?

BEN. (*Crossing away, Left.*) I feel good.

ELIZA. Has Eugene gone to the station? The midday train is due to come in.

BEN. (*Sits on bench.*) How should I know?

ELIZA. (*Calling.*) Eugene, are you up in your room? Eugene? Eugene! I'll vow, that boy! Just when I need him. (*Sees* MRS.

Pert's *knitting*.) Ben, I hope you haven't been lying around wasting time with that Mrs. Pert again?

BEN. It's the nicest time I spend.

ELIZA. I tell you what: it doesn't look right, Ben. What must the other boarders think? A woman her age—a saloon singer, a divorcee. Can't you find someone young and pretty and free to be with? I don't understand it. You're the best looking boy I've got.

BEN. If it'll make you feel better, Mama, I'll look around.

ELIZA. (*Relieved by the change in his mood, smiles. She also notices the sprawled newspaper.*) That's Mr. Clatt's newspaper. You know he's finicky about reading it first. Fold it up before you go. (EUGENE *tiptoes out the Right door.*) Eugene, where are you sneaking to? Come here.

EUGENE. Yes, Mama?

ELIZA. The midday train is due to come in. Get on down to the depot.

EUGENE. Today? I did it yesterday.

ELIZA. Every day until every room is filled. The advertising cards are on the table. Go get them. (EUGENE *exits into the house.* ELIZA *picks up flowers pots.*) I declare, seventeen is an impossible age. I don't know why he complains. He hasn't anything else to do. Spending his time up there scribbling, dreaming.

BEN. The other boarding houses send their hired help to the trains.

ELIZA. We don't have hired help, Ben Gant, you used to do it. It's little enough I've ever asked of you boys. (*To* EUGENE *who re-enters.*) Have you got the cards?

EUGENE. (*Crosses into yard.*) In my pocket.

ELIZA. (*Crosses down to* EUGENE. *Flower pots to stoop.*) Let me see them. Let me see them!

EUGENE. "Stay at Dixieland, Altamont's Homiest Boarding House." It should be homeliest.

ELIZA. Eugene!

BEN. (*Stands.*) What are you limping for? My God, those are my shoes you've got on! I threw them out yesterday!

ELIZA. They're practically brand new.

BEN. They're too small for *me*, they must be killing him.

EUGENE. Ben, please!

ELIZA. Maybe you can afford to throw out brand new shoes.

EUGENE. Ben, they're all right.

BEN. By God, it's a damned disgrace, sending him out on the streets like a hired man. Gene should be *on* that train, going to college! (BEN *sits on veranda bench.* ELIZA *proceeds to inspect flowers and place them on dining room window ledge.*)

ELIZA. That's enough—that's just enough of that! You haven't a family to provide for like I have, Ben Gant. Now I don't want to hear another word about it! Gene will go to college when we can afford it. This year he can help his Papa at the marble yard.

BEN. I thought you were going to "warm up" Papa, so he'll sell the shop.

ELIZA. Ben Gant, that wasn't intended for your ears. I'd appreciate it if you don't mention it to Mr. Gant until I have.

EUGENE. Why should Papa sell his shop?

ELIZA. Now, you're too young to worry about my business. You tend to yours.

EUGENE. What business do I have to attend to, Mama?

ELIZA. Well, get busy, get busy! Help your Papa at the shop.

EUGENE. I don't want to be a stonecutter.

ELIZA. Well, go back to the delivering newspaper business. Work for Uncle Will in his real estate office. But keep the ball rolling, child. Now, will you quit stalling and get a move on?

EUGENE. I hate drumming up trade! It's deceptive and it's begging.

ELIZA. Begging! We're not begging. We're trading. Something (*MUSIC CUE.*) for something. Tender loving care for a little cash. It's an honest living, a noble profession. The keeper of the inn, the shepherd and his flock, the Good Samaritan . . .

SONG: *"MAKE A LITTLE SUNSHINE"*

MAKE A LITTLE SUNSHINE ON SOMEONE
SPREAD A LITTLE WELCOME AROUND
TOUCH ANOTHER PERSON WITH KINDNESS
HELP A LITTLE CHIN OFF THE GROUND

TURN A LITTLE SORROW TO LAUGHTER
EV'RYBODY'S WORTH IT, IT'S TRUE

MAKE A LITTLE SUNSHINE ON SOMEONE
AND FEEL THE SUN SHINE ON YOU
    EUGENE. Oh, Mama . . .
    ELIZA. Now, listen to me.
BE A LITTLE RAINBOW FOR SOMEONE
FIND A LITTLE KITTEN A HOME
MAKE A LONELY PERSON FEEL WANTED
NO ONE OUGHT TO BE ALL ALONE

CHANGE A LITTLE GRAY SKY TO BLUE SKY
UP A LITTLE DOWN POINT OF VIEW
MAKE A LITTLE SUNSHINE ON SOMEONE
AND FEEL THE SUN SHINE ON YOU
    EUGENE.
MAKE A LITTLE SUNSHINE
    ELIZA, EUGENE.
  ON SOMEONE
BRUSH A LITTLE TEARDROP AWAY
PARCEL OUT A PINCH OF GOOD TIDING
HELP A LITTLE LAMB GONE ASTRAY

RISE UP IN THE MORNING WITH PURPOSE
THAT'S THE VERY LEAST YOU CAN DO
MAKE A LITTLE SUNSHINE ON SOMEONE
AND FEEL THE SUN SHINE ON YOU

(*Dance extension.*)

MAKE A LITTLE SUNSHINE ON SOMEONE
AND FEEL THE SUN SHINE ON YOU
    ELIZA. One more thing . . .
BUSY IS THE SURE WAY TO HAPPY
NEVER LET A DARK THOUGHT INTRUDE
TURN A BIT OF BAD LUCK
    ELIZA, BEN.
  TO GOOD LUCK
STRIKE A POSITIVE ATTITUDE
    EUGENE, BEN.
PUT A HEART IN PIECES, TOGETHER
BE A LITTLE BOTTLE OF GLUE

ELIZA, EUGENE, BEN.
MAKE A LITTLE SUNSHINE ON SOMEONE
AND FEEL THE SUN SHINE ON YOU.

(*A train whistle is heard in the distance.*)

ELIZA. Now get over to the depot right this minute. And for
heaven's sake, boy, spruce up, shoulders back! Look like you
are somebody! (EUGENE *starts off.*) And smile! Look plea-
sent! (EUGENE *grins maniacally and exits.*) What's the matter
with him, Ben? What's wrong with that boy? What's the
matter with all of you? I certainly don't know. I tell you what,
sometimes I get frightened. Seems as if everyone of you's
at the end of something, dissatisfied, and wants something
else. But it just can't be. A house divided against itself cannot stand. I'll vow, I don't know what we're coming to. Let's
not quarrel anymore. If you like, this once, as long as you're
home, why don't you eat here? I'm sure there's plenty left
over.
BEN. No, thank you, Mama.
ELIZA. A good hot meal.
BEN. (*Standing.*) I've got to get to the paper.
ELIZA. Ben, are you sure you feel all right?
BEN. (*Exiting Right.*) I feel fine.
ELIZA. Well, have a nice day at the paper, son. (*The House
Unit revolves to POSITION #3, facing full front, as* ELIZA
folds CLATT's *newspaper placing it neatly on the bench. She
turns to enter the front door, and, seeing* HELEN *with coffee
service in hand, offers assistance by holding the door.*)
HELEN. Mama, where have you been?
ELIZA. It's all right. I'm here now. (*To the* BOARDERS *who
having finished eating are entering the veranda area of the
house.*) Good afternoon. (ELIZA *exits thru front door.*)
MRS. CLATT. I ate too much again.
HELEN. (*Pouring coffee for the* BOARDERS.) Coffee, Mrs.
Clatt.
MRS. CLATT. Yes, thank you. (*To* FLORRY.) Not there!
That's my chair! That's mine since the school teacher left.
MISS BROWN. (*Blocking* FLORRY's *cross to swing.*) Oh, Mr.
Farrel, you're a teacher too, aren't you?
MR. FARREL. Of the piano. Retired.

MISS BROWN. I hope you'll stay with us for a while. Where are you from?

MR. FARREL. New York City.

MISS BROWN. You must know all the latest songs.

MR. FARREL. A few.

MISS BROWN. I'd love to learn some.

MR. FARREL. I'll tell you what— If Mrs. Pert will sing I will play right after supper.

MRS. CLATT. I don't know what Mrs. Gant makes this coffee of. There isn't a bean invented tastes like this.

JAKE. Couldn't you make it for us sometime, Helen?

HELEN. My mother always makes the coffee here. (MRS. PERT enters.)

MRS. PERT. That was scrumptious dessert, but, oh dear!

JAKE. Yes, it was good, if only the servings were bigger.

MRS. CLATT. I'm told the best boarding house food in town is down the street at Mrs. Haskell's.

JAKE. That's right, Mother. That's what I heard.

HELEN. Well, why don't you go to Mrs. Haskell's if you think you can afford to pay double?

MISS MANGLE. I spent one season there, but I prefer it here. It's more informal and entertaining.

JAKE. Not lately. It's been over a month since Mrs. Gant had to have that man Edward and his "wife" evicted for not paying their rent. She certainly loves to see the police swarm around!

MISS MANGLE. Don't you?

JAKE. I like excitement, why shouldn't I?

MISS MANGLE. Other people's excitement. Don't you want excitement of your own? I do. (LAURA JAMES, 23, carrying a suitcase and a Dixieland advertising card, enters. She is attractive, but not beautiful. She advances to the steps of the veranda.)

LAURA. Good afternoon!

JAKE. (Stands.) Good afternoon!

LAURA. Is the proprietor here?

JAKE. (Crossing towards her. Calls inside.) Mrs. Gant! Customer! (To LAURA.) Please come right up. (Leaping to LAURA.) Here let me help you. It must be awful heavy. (JAKE takes suitcase and sits it on porch. The OTHER BOARDERS look her over, whisper.)

LAURA. Thank you.

ELIZA. (*Enters from front door.*) Yes?

LAURA. Are you the proprietor?

ELIZ. Mrs. Eliza Gant—that's right.

LAURA. My name is Laura James. I found this card on the sidewalk.

ELIZA. (*Takes card.*) On the sidewalk! And you're looking for a room?

LAURA. If you have one for me.

ELIZA. Of course I have, dear—a nice quiet room. (*Makes introductions.*) Miss James, Mr. Clatt— (*Each acknowledges the introduction.*)

EUGENE. (*Urgently.*) Mama, Papa's been at Laughran's saloon again. Doctor Maguire is trying to steer him home now.

ELIZA. (*Momentarily stabbed.*) The Doctor? Is he sick or is he drunk?

EUGENE. He's rip-roaring! He's awful. He kicked Uncle Will again!

ELIZA. (*Weakly.*) I don't think I can stand it again. A new young lady, too. Oh Eugene, why do they keep bringing him home? What'll I do, child?

EUGENE. At least it's been a month this time.

W.O. GANT. (*Offstage.*) Mountain grills! Stay away from me!

JAKE. My God, Mr. Gant's on the loose again!

MISS MANGLE. Oh dear, oh dear . . .

MRS. CLATT. What? What is it?

JAKE. The old boy's on the loose again!

EUGENE. Would you go inside, all of you, please?

MRS. CLATT. I haven't finished my coffee.

EUGENE. You can wait in the parlor. Please, just until we get him upstairs!

JAKE. And miss the show?

MISS BROWN. Come along, Mr. Farrel. Let's clear the deck for the old geezer.

MR. FARREL. Perhaps there is some way I can help?

MISS BROWN. I wouldn't recommend it, Mr. Farrel.

JAKE. Look at him. He really got a snootful this time!

(EUGENE *urges several* BOARDERS *inside, where they cram in the hallway.* JAKE *and* MRS. CLATT *remain on the porch.* LAURA, *not knowing where to go, remains with* JAKE *outside.*)

W.O. GANT *clatters up the back steps, thru the door, and down the hallway his arms flailing. At heart he is a far wanderer and a minstrel but he has degraded his life with libertinism and drink. In him still, though, there is a monstrous fumbling for life. He is accompanied by* DR. MAGUIRE, *unkept but kind;* TIM LAUGHRAN, *the saloon keeper,* REED MCKINNEY *and* JOE TARKINGTON, *three cronies, disreputably dressed, also drunk but navigating.* GANT *and his companions enter the veranda area thru the front door.*)

GANT. The lowest of the low—boarding house swine! Merciful God, what a travesty! That it should come to this! (*Stumbles, almost falls, bursts into maniacal laughter.*)

EUGENE. (*Tries to take* GANT'S *arm.* GANT *flings him aside.*) Papa, come on— Papa, please!

GANT. (*Theatrically.*)
"Waken lords and ladies gay
On the mountain dawns the day—"
(*Stumbles, fall onto porch.*)

EUGENE. Okay, Papa— C'mon, grab hold of my arm. Papa, will you let me help you to your feet?

GANT. That would seem to be impossible at the moment.

SONG: *"FINGERS AND TOES"*

ONCE I HAD FINGERS AND TOES, BOY
ONCE I HAD FINGERS AND TOES
FINGERS AND TOES AND A NOSE, BOY
ONCE I HAD FINGERS AND TOES

LAST TIME I SAW THEM WAS SUNDAY
   DOWN AT TIM LAUGHRAN'S SALOON
    DRUNK AND SURLY,
   THEY STAGGERED OUT EARLY
AND I WANDERED HOME WITH THIS TUNE
  GANT & CRONIES.
ONCE I HAD EARLOBES AND LIPS, BOY
ONCE I HAD EARLOBES AND LIPS
  GANT.
PARTS THAT WERE POINTED WITH TIPS, BOY
  GANT & CRONIES.
ONCE I HAD EARLOBES AND LIPS

REED.
USELESS ANTENNAE FOR FEELIN'
GANT.
SOME FOLKS ARE BETTER OFF NUMB
HERE'S TO THE BASTARD
WHO'S HAPPILY PLASTERED
ON BOURBON, RHY WHISKEY OR RUM-
   HUMMMMM
CRONIES.
RUM, RUM, RUM . . .
GANT.
ONCE I HAD EYES THAT COULD SEE, BOY
CRONIES.
EYES THAT COULD FOCUS AND SEE
GANT.
EYES THAT CAN SEE AIN'T FOR ME, BOY
CRONIES.
ONCE I HAD EYES THAT COULD SEE
GANT.
I LIKE THE WORLD WHEN IT'S FUZZY
THAT'S WHEN IT'S RIGHT AS A ROSE
NEVER A CRISIS
WHO CARES IF THE PRICE IS
A COUPLE OF FINGERS AND TOES
CONTENT AND FORGETFUL
I WON'T BE REGRETFUL
I GOT NO FINGERS AND TOES
   GANT & CRONIES.
NO FINGERS AND TOES
NO FINGERS AND TOES
I GOT NO FINGERS AND
   GANT. (*Sinking to his knees.*)
TOES.
What am I doing here? This is not where I live. I reside at
92 Woodson Street.

   DR. MAGUIRE. Get him a drink. Maybe he'll pass out.

   GANT. Drink? Did someone say drink?

   HELEN. (*To* CRONIES.) You get out of here, now, and don't
come back till you're sober.

   ELIZA. Mr. Gant, I'd be ashamed, I'd be ashamed. I suppose
you've been to Madame Victoria's too!

   GANT. Would that I could!

HELEN. Papa! Why have you been drinking again when you know what it does to you?

GANT. Helen, I've got a pain right here.

HELEN. Of course you do. Come on, Papa. I'll put you to bed, and bring you some soup. (HELEN *manages to get* GANT *to his feet and up the steps.*)

GANT. Would you like to hear some Keats—beautiful Keats? "Ever let the fancy roam. Pleasure never is at home." (*To the* CLATTS.) Don't let me disturb your little tete-a-tete. Go right ahead. Help yourself. Another helping of mashed potatoes, Mrs. Clatt? Put another tire around your middle. (HELEN, EUGENE *and* MAGUIRE *attempt to navigate* GANT *through the house and up the stairs.*)

HELEN. We'll never get him up. He's too heavy.

DR. MAGUIRE. I guess he'll have to dry out downstairs.

ELIZA. Put him in the keeping room. (*They exit into the keeping room.* LAURA *picks up her suitcase and starts off.* ELIZA *sees her.*) Oh, Miss James. I was going to show you that room, wasn't I?

LAURA. Hmmmmmm?

ELIZA. I think you'll enjoy it here. It's quite peaceful— I'll tell you what; we don't have occurrences like this every day.

LAURA. Well, how much is it?

ELIZA. Twenty-fifteen dollars a week. Three meals a day and the use of electricity and the bath. (MR. FARREL *exits house with suitcase.*) Mr. Farrel, you paid for a week in advance. (MR. FARREL *shrugs, returns to house.*) Do you want me to show it to you?

LAURA. No, I'm sure it will be all right.

ELIZA. That's in advance, that is.

LAURA. Well as long as you're sure it's generally quiet and peaceful here. (*Opens her purse, takes out a roll of one-dollar bills, puts them one by one into* ELIZA'S *outstretched hand.*) One, two, three— I always keep my money in one-dollar bills —it feels like it's more.

ELIZA. (*Almost cheerful again.*) Oh, I know what you mean.

LAURA. . . . Nine . . . ten . . .

BEN. (*Enters Right.*) I heard about Papa—how is he? (*Crosses to porch.*)

ELIZA. Drunk. Dr. Maguire's taking care of him now. Ben,

this is Miss James—this is my son, Ben Gant. (BEN, *impressed by her looks, nods.*)

LAURA. —fourteen, fifteen. There.

ELIZA. (*Puts the money in bosom of her dress.*) Thank you, dear. Miss James is going to stay with us a while, we hope! I'll take you up, dear. You'll be cozy and comfortable here. (*They start inside.*) I'll show you the rest of the house later.

LAURA. (*Turning in doorway.*) Nice to have met you, Mr. Gant. (ELIZA *and* LAURA *exit thru the front door.* MAGUIRE *returns. During the following scene we are aware of* LAURA *as she inspects and settles into her new room upstairs.*)

DR. MAGUIRE. Your sister can handle that old goat like a lamb.

BEN. Is he all right?

DR. MAGUIRE. (*Crosses to yard.*) He will be. He will be.

BEN. Maguire (*Crosses to yard.*), can I speak to you a minute about me? If you have a minute. (EUGENE *enters and watches.*)

DR. MAGUIRE. Shoot, Ben.

BEN. (*To* EUGENE.) Haven't you got something else to do?

EUGENE. (*Innocently.*) No.

BEN. (*To* DOCTOR.) I suppose you've heard there's a war going on in Europe. (*Pause.*) I've decided to enlist in Canada.

EUGENE. (*Rises.*) What do you want to do that for?

BEN. (*To* EUGENE.) You keep out of this.

DR. MAGUIRE. It's a good question, Ben. Do you want to save this world? This world?

BEN. In Christ's name, Maguire, you'll recommend me, won't you? You examined me just a couple of months ago.

DR. MAGUIRE. (*Crosses, puts down his bag on tree swing.*) Well, let's see, for a war the requirements are somewhat different. Stick out your chest. (BEN *does so; the* DOCTOR *looks him over.*) Feet? Good arch. How're your teeth, son?

BEN. Aren't you overdoing it, Doc? (BEN *draws his lips and shows two rows of hard white grinders. Unexpectedly* MAGUIRE *prods* BEN'S *distended solar plexus with a strong finger and* BEN'S *distended chest collapses. He sinks to the veranda edge, coughing.*)

EUGENE. What did you do that for?

DR. MAGUIRE. (*Crosses for bag.*) They'll have to save this world without you, Ben.

BEN. (*Rises, grabs the* DOCTOR.) What do you mean? (HELEN *enters with broom and begins to straighten area.*)

DR. MAGUIRE. That's all. That's all.

BEN. You're saying I'm not all right?

DR. MAGUIRE. (*Turns to him.*) Who said you weren't all right?

BEN. Quit your kidding.

DR. MAGUIRE. What's the rush? We may get into this war ourselves before too long. Wait a bit. (*To* EUGENE.) Isn't that right, son? (*Turns for bag.*)

BEN. Maguire (*Grabs his arm.*), I want to know. Am I all right or not?

DR. MAGUIRE. Yes, Ben, you're all right. Why, you're one of the most all right people I know. (*Carefully as he feels* BEN'S *arm.*) You're a little run down, that's all. You need some meat on those bones. (BEN *breaks from him, moves away Right to* HELEN, *takes coffee cup from tray.*) You can't exist with a cup of coffee in one hand and a cigarette in the other. Besides, the Altamont air is good for you. Stick around. Deep breaths, Ben, deep breaths. (*Picks up his bag.*) Take it easy. Try not to care too much. (*Exits.*)

EUGENE. (*Crosses to Right of* BEN.) He's right, you know. You ought to try to look after yourself more, Ben. (*Tries to comfort* BEN. BEN *avoids his touch, lurches away.*)

BEN. He doesn't have any spirit about this war, that's all that's the matter with him.

EUGENE. I didn't know you wanted to get away from here so badly.

BEN. (*Looks over at* EUGENE. *Crosses to yard.*) Come here, you little bum. (EUGENE *backs away playfully.*) My God, haven't you got a clean shirt you can wear? (*He gets out some money.*) Here, take this and go get that damn long hair cut off, and get some shoes that fit, for God's sake, you look like a lousy tramp—

EUGENE. (*Crossing Right of* BEN.) Ben, I can't keep taking money from you.

BEN. What else have you got me for? (*The brothers roughhouse,* EUGENE *giggling. Then with sudden intense ferocity* BEN *seizes* EUGENE's *arms, shakes him.*) You listen to me. You go to college, understand? Don't you settle for anyone or anything—learn your lesson from me! I'm a hack writer on a hick paper— I'll never be anything else. You can be, Gene.

Get money out of them, any way you can! Beg it, take it, steal it, but get it from them somehow. Get it and get the hell away from them. To hell with them all! (BEN *coughs.* EUGENE *tries to help him.* BEN *escapes him, sits tiredly on veranda's edge.*) I didn't make it. But you can, Gene. I let her hold on and hold on until it was too late. Don't you let that happen to you. And Gene, don't try to please everybody—just please yourself. (BEN *realizes* EUGENE's *confusion. Noticing* LAURA's *hat, points to it.*) Where's she from?

EUGENE. (*Picks up hat, sniffs it, puts it on.*) I don't know. I don't even know her name.

BEN. Miss James. I'll have to note her arrival in my "society" column. (*Takes hat from* EUGENE, *admires it.*) The firm young line of spring—budding, tender, virginal, "Like something swift, with wings, which hovers in a wood—among the feathery trees, suspected, but uncaught, unseen." Exquisite. (*Returns hat to table.*) C'mon, follow me downtown. I'll buy you a cup of mocha.

EUGENE. Maybe I ought to stick around here for a while.

BEN. With her around, I don't blame you. I dream of elegant women myself, all the time. (MRS. PERT *enters, overhears, crosses Right for knitting.*)

EUGENE. You do? But, Ben, if you dream of elegant women, how is it, well—

BEN. (*Goes to* FATTY.) Fatty? Fatty's a happy woman—there's no pain in her that she feels she has to unload onto somebody else. Besides, she's adorable as a duck; don't you think so? (MRS. PERT *exits into house.*)

SONG: *"FATTY"*

SHE STOLE MY HEART
RIGHT FROM THE START
SHE'S BEEN MY FAV'RITE PAL
SHE MAKES ME SMILE
SHE'S JUST MY STYLE
I LOVE THAT BIG OL' BOUNCY GAL

I CALL HER FATTY
SHE DOESN'T CARE
SHE KNOWS SHE SUITS ME FINE

SHE'S PLUMP AND TENDER
AND EV'RY INCH IS MINE, MINE, MINE, MINE

I'M GLAD I FOUND HER
SHE'S SWEET AND KIND
AND JUST THE PERFECT SIZE
I LOVE MY FATTY
SHE LIGHTS THE LOVE-LITE IN MY EYES

SHE SPARKLES LIKE THE MORNIN' DEW
    SHININ' IN THE SUN
AND WHEN I TAKE MY SUGAR'S HAND
I FEEL OUR HEARTS BECOME AS ONE

I'D EVEN WANT HER
IF SHE WERE THIN
AND STYLISH TO THE EYE
I CALL HER FATTY
AND IF I'M LUCKY
SHE'LL BE MY FATTY
    TILL I DIE
AND IF I'M LUCKY
SHE'LL BE MY FATTY
    TILL I DIE.
C'mon. Follow me downtown. I'm gonna buy you a clean shirt.

ACT ONE

SCENE 2

That evening. The action is continuous. BOARDERS *enter the parlor area as the House Unit revolves back to POSITION #1, wide view.*

MRS. SNOWDEN. Don't you just love this evening mountain air? It's so cool and refreshing.
MRS. CLATT. It bothers the dickens out of my rheumatism.
FLORRY. How do you like my new dress, Mr. Clatt?
JAKE. Have you seen Miss James?
MISS BROWN. Oh, Mr. Farrel, no more excuses now. Mrs. Pert said she would sing, won't you, Mrs. Pert, if you'll play.

Mr. Farrel. All right, all right. Come along, Mrs. Pert, do
you see anything here that suits you?
Fatty. No! I'm teasing. This piece, here—one of my fa-
vorites. In D-flat.
Mr. Farrel. E-flat?
Fatty. No, no, D-flat. They just loved this down at the
saloon.

SONG: *"ASTORIA GLORIA"*

A LONESOME, BROADWAY JOHNNY
   SAT CRYIN' IN HIS ROOM
PINING FOR A BUDDING LOVE
   JUST ABOUT TO BLOOM:
HE GAZED BEYOND HIS WINDOW
   UP TO THE SILVERY MOON
AND SOON THE NEIGHBORS HEARD POOR
   JOHNNY
   CROON THIS MOURNFUL TUNE

ASTORIA GLORIA
GIRL OF MY DREAMS
WHY DO YOU HAVE TO LIVE
   WAY OUT IN QUEENS
GEE LIFE WOULD BE EASIER
   DON'T YOU AGREE
IF YOU COULD BE CLOSER TO ME

EUPHORIA, GLORIA
DEAR, IT WOULD BE
LET'S GET TO CHANGIN' YOUR
   PROXIMITY
OH, I COULD SEE MORE A' YA
WHAT A DELIGHT
CLOSER TO YOU NIGHT AFTER NIGHT

WHAT KIND OF CHANCE
HAVE WE TO GET
   THIS ROMANCE GROWIN'
WHEN ALL I DO
IS SPEND MY TIME
   COMIN' AND GOIN'

LET'S TELL YOUR MA, AND GET
   MARRIED TODAY
TELL HER YOU'RE LEAVIN', HEY!
WHAT DO YOU SAY—
ASTORIA, GLORIA
LOVE OF MY DREAMS
PRITTIEST GIRL IN QUEENS
YOU'RE THE PRITTIEST GIRL IN QUEENS.

(*Dance extension.*)

FATTY & BOARDERS.
ASTORIA, GLORIA
WHAT DO YOU SAY
LET'S TELL YOUR MA, AND GET
   MARRIED TODAY
ASTORIA, GLORIA
LOVE OF MY DREAMS
PRITTIEST GIRL IN QUEENS
PRITTIEST GIRL, PRITTIEST GIRL
PRITTIEST GIRL IN QUEENS.

(FATTY *and the* BOARDERS *exit.* EUGENE *enters, sees* LAURA'S *hat, and is examining it when* LAURA *enters from the house.*)

LAURA. Good evening.
EUGENE. What!
LAURA. I said good evening.
EUGENE. Goodyado.
LAURA. I beg your pardon?
EUGENE. I meant to say good evening, how do you do?
LAURA. Goodyado! I like that much better. Goodyado! (*She extends her hand.* EUGENE, *embarrassed, hangs her hat on it and crosses Left.* LAURA *following.*) Don't you think that's funny?
EUGENE. (*Sitting on swing.*) It's about as funny as most things I do.
LAURA. May I sit down?
EUGENE. (*He rises, they sit.*) Please.
LAURA. I'm Laura James.
EUGENE. I know. I'm Eugene Gant.
LAURA. You know, I've seen you before.

EUGENE. Yes, earlier this afternoon.

LAURA. I mean before that. I saw you throw those advertising cards in the gutter.

EUGENE. You did?

LAURA. I was coming from the station. You know where the train crosses the street? You were just standing there staring at it. I walked right by you and smiled at you. I never got such a snub before in my whole life. My, you must be crazy about trains.

EUGENE. You stood right beside me?

LAURA. Yes, I did.

EUGENE. Where are you from?

LAURA. Richmond, Virginia.

EUGENE. Richmond! That's a big city, isn't it?

LAURA. It's pretty big.

EUGENE. You have a big library. Did you know it has over a hundred thousand books in it?

LAURA. No, I didn't know that.

EUGENE. Well, it does. I read that somewhere. It would take a long time to read a hundred thousand books, wouldn't it?

LAURA. Yes, it would.

EUGENE. I figure about twenty years. How many books do they let you take out at one time?

LAURA. I really don't know.

EUGENE. They only let you take out two here! (LAURA *laughs.*) Are you laughing at me?

LAURA. Of course not.

EUGENE. You are smiling a lot!

LAURA. I'm smiling because I'm enjoying myself. I like talking to you.

EUGENE. I like talking to you, too. I always talk better with older people.

LAURA. Oh!

EUGENE. They know so much more.

LAURA. Like me?

EUGENE. Yes. You're very interesting.

LAURA. (*Rises, a step Right.*) Am I?

EUGENE. Oh yes! You're very interesting! (JAKE CLATT *approaches, from Right.*)

JAKE. Miss James?

LAURA. Yes, Mr. Platt?

JAKE. Clatt.

LAURA. Clatt.

JAKE. Jake Clatt! It's a lovely evening. Would you like to take a stroll?

LAURA. It feels to me like it's going to rain.

JAKE. (*Looking at sky.*) Oh, I don't know.

EUGENE. (*Rising.*) It's going to rain, all right.

JAKE. Oh, I wouldn't be so sure!

LAURA. Perhaps some other time, Mr. Clatt.

JAKE. Certainly. Good night, Miss James. Good night, sonny. (EUGENE *glares after* JAKE, *who exits Right. A train whistle moans mournfully in the distance.* EUGENE *cocks an ear, listens.*)

LAURA. You do like trains, don't you?

EUGENE. Mama took us on one to St. Louis to the Fair, when I was only five. Have you ever touched one?

LAURA. What?

EUGENE. A locomotive. Have you ever put your hand on one? You have to touch things to understand them.

LAURA. Aren't they rather hot?

EUGENE. Even a cold one, standing in the station yard. You know what you feel? (*MUSIC CUE.*) You feel the shining steel rails under it . . . and the rails send a message right through your fingertips . . . a message of all the faraway places that engine ever passed. Places you don't even know, can hardly imagine. You feel the rhythm of a whole life, a whole country clicking through your hand.

SONG: *"RAILBIRD"*

HERE COMES ENGINE NINETY NINE
PRIDE OF ALL THE SEABOARD LINE
SLOWIN' DOWN TO PULL THE GRADE
ONE JUMP NOW AND I'LL HAVE IT MADE—

RAILBIRD RAILBIRD
WISH I WERE A RAILBIRD
WEDDED TO A WHISTLE, IRON AND STEAM
RAILBIRD RAILBIRD
IF I WERE A RAILBIRD
I COULD SEE THE CITIES I SEE IN MY DREAMS
THE MOUNTAINS AND THE VALLEYS, THE
       RIVERS AND STREAMS

YARD BOSS LOOK THE OTHER WAY
RAILBIRD RIDES BUT HE DON'T PAY
SWITCHMAN, BRAKEMAN, GREEN OR RED
   NEW YORK CITY IS DEAD AHEAD

RAILBIRD RAILBIRD
WISH I WERE A RAILBIRD
WEDDED TO A WHISTLE, IRON AND STEAM
RAILBIRD RAILBIRD
IF I WERE A RAILBIRD
I COULD SEE THE CITIES I SEE IN MY DREAMS
THE MOUNTAINS AND THE VALLEYS, THE
   RIVERS AND STREAMS

DOZIN' ON A FLATCAR
DREAMIN' ON MY BACK
FEELIN' THE WHEELS, GO
   CLICKETY-CLACK
LISTEN TO THE PISTONS
   USIN' UP THE COAL
EV'RY LOVIN' MILE LIBERATES MY SOUL—

MAYBE I'LL JUST HEAD OUT WEST
ANYWHERE I THINK IS BEST
BOXCAR CHARLIE, SHARE SOME WINE?
CASEY JONES WAS A FRIEND OF MINE

RAILBIRD RAILBIRD
WISH I WERE A RAILBIRD
WEDDED TO A WHISTLE, IRON AND STEAM
RAILBIRD RAILBIRD
IF I WERE A RAILBIRD
I COULD SEE THE CITIES I SEE IN MY DREAMS
THE MOUNTAINS AND THE VALLEYS, THE
   RIVERS AND STREAMS
I WONDER WHAT THE FOLKS ARE LIKE
   DOWN IN NEW ORLEANS?

LAURA. (*Impressed.*) If I touched you now, would it help me to understand you—even if you're not a locomotive? (*She reaches to touch his hand. He is excited and becomes flustered.*)

EUGENE. (*Rises.*) I'll get us some lemonade. (*He exits into the house.*)

SONG: *"IF I EVER LOVED HIM"*

LAURA.
THE BOY SHOULD BE JUST A DISTRACTION
EASY ENOUGH TO RESIST
YET I FEEL THE STRANGEST ATTRACTION
THAT KNOWS ONLY HOW TO PERSIST

GENTLY AS AN EARLY MORNING WHISPER
ROUGHLY AS A PATCH OF SCRATCHY WHISKER
WONDER HOW HE'D LOVE ME
IF I EVER LOVED HIM

LIGHTLY AS A DISTANT CHURCHBELL TOLLING
HEAVY AS A CLAP OF THUNDER ROLLING
WONDER HOW HE'D LOVE ME
IF I EVER LOVED HIM

HURRIED OR PATIENT
TIMID OR FREE
SELFISH OR HAPPY TO SHARE
TRUSTING OR JEALOUS
HOW WOULD HE BE
AND JUST HOW MUCH DO I CARE

COULD IT BE MY HEART HAS MADE ITS MIND
    UP
    AND IT'S ONLY TIME UNTIL I WIND UP
        HOPELESSLY ENAMORED
            AND LONGING TO SAY—
    IF I EVER LOVED HIM
COULD I EVER LOVE HIM
    MORE THAN I LOVE HIM TODAY?
MORE THAN I LOVE HIM TODAY
MORE THAN I LOVE HIM TODAY

(LAURA *embraces the door post as the House Unit revolves to* POSITION #4 *revealing the keeping room where* GANT *lies motionless on a couch.* ELIZA *enters thru the door, Right, with pitcher of water, drinking glass, pillow and blanket. She switches on wall sconce.*)

GANT. Helen?

ELIZA. (*Bitterly.*) No, it's not Helen, Mr. Gant. (ELIZA *pours glass of water. Without turning, she leaves glass and pitcher on dresser.*)

GANT. If that's water, take it away.

ELIZA. Why aren't you asleep? Do you have any pain?

GANT. None but the everyday pain of thinking. You wouldn't know what that is.

ELIZA. I wouldn't know?

GANT. How could you? You're always too busy puttering.

ELIZA. Oh, now that's a good one. All the work I do around here, and you call it puttering?

GANT. Some people are doers, some are thinkers.

ELIZA. (*Placing pillow under* GANT's *head.*) Somebody has to *do*, Mr. Gant. Somebody has to. Oh! I know you look on yourself as some kind of artistic fella—but personally, a man who has to be brought maudlin through the streets—screaming curses—if you call that artistic!

GANT. The hell hound is at it again. Shut up, woman!

ELIZA. (*Straightening bedsheet.*) Mr. Gant, I came in here to see if there was something I could do for you. Now will you please turn over and look at me when I talk to you? You know I can't stand being turned away from.

GANT. You're a bloody monster, you would drink my heart's blood!

ELIZA. You don't mean that—we've come this far together; I guess we can continue to the end. (*Covers him with blanket.*) You know I was thinking only this morning about that first day we met. Do you realize it was thirty-one years ago, come July?

GANT. (*Groaning.*) Merciful God, thirty-one long miserable years!

ELIZA. (*Picking up jacket from floor, inspecting.*) I can remember it like it was yesterday. I passed by your shop and there you were. I'll vow you looked as big as one of your tombstones—and as dusty—with a wild and dangerous look in your eye. You were romantic in those days—like the fellow says, a regular courtin' fool—"Miss Pentland," you said, "you have come into this hot and grubby shop like a cooling summer shower." That's just what you said!

GANT. And you've been a wet blanket ever since.

ELIZA. (*Crossing Right for sewing basket.*) I forgive you

your little jokes, Mr. Gant. I forgive your little jokes. (*She sits Right mending his jacket.*)

GANT. (*Slowly turns and finally looks at her.*) Do you? Do you ever forgive me, Eliza? If I could make you understand something. I was dozing just now, dreaming of the past. The far past. The people and the place I came from. Those great barns of Pennsylvania. The order, the thrift, the plenty. It all started out so right, there. There I was a man who set out to get order and position in life. And what have I come to? Only rioting and confusion, searching and wandering. There was so much before, so much. Now it's all closing in. My God, Eliza, where has it all gone? Why am I here, now, at the rag end of my life? The years are all blotted and blurred—my youth a red waste—I've gotten old, an old man. But why here? Why here?

ELIZA. (*Rises to him, adjusting blanket.*) You belong here, Mr. Gant, that's why! You belong here.

GANT. And as I get weaker and weaker, you get stronger and stronger.

ELIZA. Pshaw! If you feel that way, it's because you have no position in life. If you'd ever listened to me once, things would have been different. You didn't believe me, did you (*Resumes mending at chair Right.*), when I told you that little, old marble shop of yours would be worth a fortune some day? Will and I happened to be downtown this morning— (GANT *groans.*) and old Mr. Beecham from the bank stopped us on the street and he said, "Mrs. Gant, the bank is looking for a site to build a big new office building, and do you know the one we have our eye on?" And I said, "No." "We have our eye on Mr. Gant's shop, and we're willing to pay twenty thousand dollars for it!" Now what do you think of that? (*She sits and starts to mend robe.*)

GANT. And you came in here with only pity in your heart!

ELIZA. Well, I'll tell you what, twenty thousand dollars is a lot of money!

GANT. And my angel, my Carrara angel? You were going to sell her too?

ELIZA. The angel, the angel, the angel! I'm so tired of hearing about that angel!

GANT. You always have been. Money dribbled from your honeyed lips. But never a word about my angel. I've started twenty pieces of marble trying to capture her. But my life's work doesn't interest you.

ELIZA. (*Crosses to head of couch.*) If you haven't been able to do it in all these years, don't you think your gift as a stone-cutter may be limited?

GANT. Yes, Mrs. Gant, it may be limited. It may be limited.

ELIZA. Then why don't you sell the shop? We can pay off the mortgage at Dixieland and then just set back big as you please and live off the income from the boarders the rest of our lives!

GANT. (*Furiously, almost leaping out of bed. ELIZA backs off.*) Oh, holy hell. Wow-ee! The boarders! That parade of incognito pimps and prostitutes, calling themselves penniless piano salesmen, pining widows, part-time teachers and God knows what all! Woman, have mercy! That shop is my last refuge on earth. I beg you—let me die in peace! You won't have long to wait. You can do what you please with it after I'm gone. But give me a little comfort now. *And leave me my work!* (*He sentimentally seeks the plump pillow.*)

ELIZA. Mr. Gant, I guess I never will understand you. I guess that's just the way it is. Good night. Try to get some sleep. I reckon it's like the fellow says, some people never get to understand each other—not in this life. (*ELIZA exits.*)

GANT. Oh-h-h, I curse the day I was ever given life by that blood-thirsty monster up above. Oh-h-h, Jesus! I beg of you. I know I've been bad. Forgive me. Have mercy and pity upon me. Give me another chance in Jesus' name . . . oh-h-h! (*GANT covers his head with bedsheet as the House Unit revolves to POSITION #2. BEN and FATTY are seated on floor of the veranda drinking beer. BEN is playing his ukelele.*)

FATTY. You know that's the second time we've been to the store for beer.

BEN. Well, drink up. We'll make it three.

FATTY. Ben Gant, you are a reckless man.

BEN. Listen to her, reckless.

FATTY. Honey, I cannot let you spend all your money on me. You got to start thinking some about saving for tomorrow.

BEN. Fatty, I don't give a damn about tomorrow. Besides, saving's for squirrels.

SONG: *"A DIME AIN'T WORTH A NICKEL"*

A DIME AIN'T WORTH
A NICKEL TO ME
A NICKEL AIN'T WORTH A CENT
A DOLLAR SAVED
IS A GOOD TIME LOST
A DOLLAR SHOULD BE SPENT
   BUYIN' MERRIMENT

A BUCK WON'T PLACE
A SMILE ON YOUR FACE
DEPOSITED IN A DRAWER
A COIN MY FRIEND
IS A JOY TO SPEND
OR LEND THE GUY NEXT DOOR
   WHAT'S A DOLLAR FOR

PAY DAY, I'M LIKE A MILLIONAIRE
BY MONDAY MORNING I'M BROKE
GREENJACK, GREEN IS A FICKLE THING
AND LIFE IS JUST A JOKE

A DIME AIN'T WORTH
A NICKEL TO ME
A DOLLAR AIN'T WORTH A HALF
SO DON'T PUT YOUR SWEAT IN A SAVINGS BANK
INVEST IT ALL IN A LAUGH, HA!
INVEST IT ALL IN A LAUGH
   FATTY.
A BUCK WON'T PLACE
A SMILE ON YOUR FACE
DEPOSITED IN A DRAWER
YOU CAN'T MISBEHAVE
WHEN YOU'RE IN YOUR GRAVE
OR CHASE THE BOY NEXT DOOR
   BEN & FATTY.
WHEN YOU'RE EIGHTY-FOUR

PAY DAY, I'M LIKE A MILLIONAIRE
BY MONDAY MORNIN' I'M BROKE

GREENJACK, GREEN IS A FICKLE THING
AND LIFE IS JUST A JOKE

A DIME AIN'T WORTH
A NICKEL TO ME
A DOLLAR AIN'T WORTH A HALF
SO DON'T PUT YOUR SWEAT IN A SAVINGS BANK
INVEST IT ALL IN A LAUGH, HA!
INVEST IT ALL IN A LAUGH

(*Dance Extension.*)

BEN & FATTY.
SO DON'T PUT YOUR SWEAT IN A SAVINGS BANK
INVEST IT ALL IN A LAUGH, HA!
INVEST IT ALL IN A LAUGH.

(BEN & FATTY *exit Right.* EUGENE *and* LAURA *enter from the house, with lemonade glasses.*)

EUGENE. How long do you plan to stay here—?

LAURA. How old are you, Gene?

EUGENE. I'm sorry, please—

LAURA. No, you.

EUGENE. How long do you plan to stay here, Miss James?

LAURA. (*Crosses Right, sits on swing.*) My name is Laura. I wish you'd call me that.

EUGENE. (*Follows, sits to her Right.*) Laura. That's a lovely name. Do you know what it means?

LAURA. No.

EUGENE. I read a book once on the meaning of names. Laura is the laurel. The Greek symbol of victory.

LAURA. Victory. Maybe some day I'll live up to that! What does Eugene mean?

EUGENE. Oh, I forget.

LAURA. You, forget?

EUGENE. It means "well born."

LAURA. How old are you, Eugene?

EUGENE. Why?

LAURA. (*Rises, crosses behind swing.*) I'm always curious about people's ages. I'm twenty-one. You?

EUGENE. Nineteen. Will you be staying here long?

LAURA. (*Crossing Right.*) I don't know exactly.

EUGENE. (*Rises, following.*) You're only twenty-one?

LAURA. How old did you think I was?

EUGENE. Oh, about that. About twenty-one, I'd say. That's not old at all.

LAURA. (*Laughs.*) I don't feel it is!

EUGENE. I was afraid you might think I was too young for you to waste time with me like this!

LAURA. (*Crossing to him.*) I don't think nineteen is young at all!

EUGENE. (*They almost collide in their excitement.*) No, it isn't really, is it? (*MUSIC CUE.*)

LAURA. Gene, if we keep rushing together like this, we're going to have a collision. (*They laugh, pause, she waits for him to kiss her. He doesn't. She kisses him and runs into the house.*)

SONG: *"I GOT A DREAM TO SLEEP ON"*

EUGENE.
JUST HAD THE PERFECT ENDING
    TO A VERY SPECIAL DAY
GOTTA PLEASANT DREAM TO DREAM, SO
    SANDMAN WON'T YOU BLOW
        A LITTLE SAND MY WAY

SET OUT MY PAJAMAS
MAKE MY BED UP RIGHT
I GOT A DREAM TO SLEEP ON
I FELL IN LOVE TONIGHT

I JUST KISSED AN ANGEL
SHE JUST HELD ME TIGHT
I GOT A DREAM TO SLEEP ON
I FELL IN LOVE TONIGHT

SHE WAS TENDER
I WAS GENTLE
SHE WAS FAR FROM TEMPER'MENTAL
SHE GOT COMFY
I GOT COZY
NOW MY FUTURE'S LOOKIN' ROSY

SO NOBODY WAKE ME
ONCE I DIM THE LIGHT
I GOT A DREAM TO SLEEP ON
I FELL IN LOVE TONIGHT

(*Dance extension.*)

SO NOBODY WAKE ME
ONCE I DIM THE LIGHT
I GOT A DREAM TO SLEEP ON
I FELL IN LOVE TONIGHT.

(EUGENE *falls into swing, Left. House Unit to POSITION #1.* BEN *and* FATTY *return, Right, with more beer.*)

FATTY. You have really extended yourself tonight. Is this beer imported?
BEN. Listen to her, imported. From Milwaukee. (ELIZA *enters veranda area from side door.*)
FATTY. 'Evening, Mrs. Gant. Why don't you sit down and join us for a while?
ELIZA. (*Begins picking up bottles.*) I've told you before, Mrs. Pert, I don't tolerate drinking at Dixieland!
BEN. Oh, Mama, for God's sake—
ELIZA. You two can be heard all over the house with your carrying on.
BEN. Listen to her! Carrying on—
ELIZA. As I passed your door just now, Mrs. Pert, there was a light under it. If you're going to spend all night out here, there's no sense in wasting electricity.
BEN. The Lord said "Let there be light," even if it's only 40 watt.
ELIZA. (*Crosses Left to him.*) Don't you get on your high horse with me, Ben Gant. You've squandered every penny you've ever earned because you've never known the value of a dollar!
BEN. The value of a dollar! Oh what the hell's the use of it, anyway? Come on, Fatty, let's go for a stroll. (BEN *crosses down steps Left.* EUGENE *crosses up steps, sees* LAURA *about to enter porch from front door.*)
FATTY. (*Rises.*) Whatever you say, Ben, old Fatty's willing.
ELIZA. (*Attacking* FATTY.) Mrs. Pert, I don't want any

butt-ins from you, do you understand? You're just a paying boarder here. That's all. You're not a member of my family, and never will be, no matter what low methods you try. (FATTY *crosses Left to* BEN.)

EUGENE. Mama, please.

ELIZA. I'm only trying to keep decency and order here, and this is the thanks I get! You should all get down on your knees and be grateful to me!

BEN. What am I supposed to be grateful for, Mama? For what?

FATTY. (*Trying to stop it.*) Ben, Ben, come on.

BEN. (*Crossing up steps to* ELIZA.) For selling the house that Papa built with his two hands and moving us into this drafty barn where we share our roof, our food, our pleasures, our privacy so that you can be Queen Bee? Is that what I'm supposed to be grateful for?

ELIZA. (*Picks up bottle and glasses.*) It's that vile liquor that's talking!

EUGENE. (*Between them.*) Let's stop it! For God's sake, let's stop it! Mama, go to bed, please. Ben—

BEN. Look at your kid there! You've had him out on the streets since he was eight years old—collecting bottles, selling papers—anything that would bring in a penny.

ELIZA. Gene is old enough to earn his keep!

BEN. Then he's old enough for you to let go of him! But no, you'd rather hang on to him like a piece of property! Maybe he'll grow in value, you can turn a quick trade on him, make a profit on him. He isn't a son, he's an investment! (ELIZA *slaps* BEN. *There is a long silence.*) Come on, Fatty. (BEN *exits past* FATTY *down Left.*)

FATTY. He didn't mean it, Mrs. Gant. (*She follows* BEN.) Ben? Ben, wait for Fatty! (*Exits.*)

EUGENE. (*Quietly, miserably; crosses to* ELIZA.) Mama. Mama. Mama!

ELIZA. (*Pulling away.*) Well, she put him up to it! He never used to talk to me like that. You stood right there and saw it. Now I'll ask you, was it my fault? Well, was it?

EUGENE. (*Looks after* LAURA.) Mama, Mama, in God's name forget about it and go to bed.

ELIZA. (*Crosses to porch, puts glasses on tray.*) All of you. Every single one of you. Your father, then Ben, now you— you all blame me. And not one of you has any idea, any idea

—you don't know what I've had to put up with all these years. (*Sits on bench.*) I've done the best I could. Your father's never given me a moment's peace. Nobody knows what I've been through with him. Nobody knows, child, nobody knows.

EUGENE. (*Sits Left of her.*) I know, Mama. I do know. Forget about it! It's all right.

ELIZA. You just can't realize. Ben and I used to be so close —I don't think a mother and son were ever closer when he was younger. The little notes he was always writing me . . . I'd find them slipped under my door, when he got up early to go on his paper route . . . "Good morning, Mama!" . . . "Have a nice day, Mama." We were so close . . .

EUGENE. (*Gently.*) It's late. You're tired.

ELIZA. (*Managing to pull herself together. Rises.*) Well, like the fellow says, it's no use crying over *that* spilt milk. I have all those napkins and towels to iron for tomorrow. I'm not going to spend my life slaving away here for a bunch of boarders. One of these days you may just find us Gants living in a big house in Doak Park. I've got the lot—the best lot out there. Well—I'd better get at those napkins. Are you coming in, child? (*Rises.*)

EUGENE. (*Rises.*) In a little while.

ELIZA. Don't forget to turn off the sign. Good night, son. (*Sits, kisses EUGENE.*) Get a good night's sleep, boy. You mustn't neglect your health. Good night, son. (*She starts in.*)

EUGENE. Don't work too late.

ELIZA. Gene, you know where Sunset Terrace runs up the hill? At the top of the rise? That's my lot. You know where I mean, don't you?

EUGENE. Yes, Mama.

ELIZA. And that's where we'll build—right on the very top. I made a map of it. I'll get it and show you.

EUGENE. Yes, Mama. Now, for God's sake, go and finish your work so you can get to sleep!

ELIZA. It'll only take a minute. (ELIZA *exits into house.* LAURA *enters from front door. She crosses Right to* EUGENE.)

EUGENE. You heard all that. I'm sorry.

LAURA. You don't have to apologize. Let's take a walk and not tell Mr. Flatt.

EUGENE. Clatt.

LAURA. Oh, Clatt. (*They exit Left.*)

ELIZA. (*Enters.*) See, looky here—Sunset Terrace runs up—

(*She looks around.*) Gene? Eugene? Gene, I asked you to turn out that sign! That boy. I don't know what I'm going to do with him. (*Goes into the hall, turns out the sign and stands for a moment.* ELIZA *comes down to the edge of the veranda and looks out into the night in the direction taken by* BEN *and* FATTY.) Ben? Ben? (*MUSIC CUE.*) Where are you, Ben? There's never anybody here when I need them. (ELIZA *sits on porch stoop.*)

SONG: *"DRIFTING"*

PEOPLE ARE LIKE PETALS
   PUT UPON A POND
DRIFTING, DRIFTING, DRIFTING
LILIES BY A LAKE SIDE
   TOUCHING AT THE START
      THEN DRIFTING, DRIFTING
      APART

EACH OF US A BLOSSOM
   SET UPON A STREAM
DRIFTING, DRIFTING, DRIFTING
AUTUMN LEAVES OF COLOR
   WEEDED AT THE START
      THEN DRIFTING, DRIFTING
      APART.

WHO KNOWS WHERE THE CURRENT
   WILL TAKE ME
WHO KNOWS WHERE THE CURRENT
   WILL TAKE YOU
YOU NEVER MEANT TO FORSAKE ME
I NEVER MEANT TO FORSAKE YOU

EV'RY SOUL, A SAILOR
   SAILING OUT TO SEA
DRIFTING, DRIFTING, DRIFTING,
NESTLED CLOSE TOGETHER
   SAFELY AT THE START
      THEN DRIFTING, DRIFTING,
      APART.

CURTAIN

ACT TWO

Scene 1

Gant's *marble shop, a week later.* Gant's *office is Left, his work area Right, and the entrance to the shop, Left Center. Slabs of granite, a couchant lamb, an Egyptian urn, and tools fill the area. The largest and most prominent monument is a delicately carved angel of lustrous white Carrara marble, with an especially beautiful smiling countenance. It stands Right of the entrance. To the Left is a smaller copy of the angel which* Gant *created. As the curtain rises* Eugene *is sweeping the floor, Right. After a moment,* Gant *enters.*

Eugene. Papa, Mama was just here. She was looking for you.

Gant. I know. I've been sitting over at Laughran's saloon waiting for her to leave. (*He exits into office and returns with work apron.*)

Eugene. She had on her dealing and bargaining outfit.

Gant. (*Crossing Right to work table.*) And she said she'd be back.

Eugene. Yes.

Gant. I have a mind what she's up to. She'll be back with freshly drawn up papers tucked in her bosom. Yes, when you touch the breast of Miss Eliza you feel the sharp crackle of bills of sale.

Eugene. Papa, you were young when you got married, weren't you?

Gant. What?

Eugene. When did you get married?

Gant. It was thirty-one bitter years ago when your mother first came wriggling around that corner at me like a snake on her belly— (Madame Victoria, *the town madame, enters. She is well-clad, carries herself stylishly.* Gant *rises.*) Victoria, Madame Victoria! Well this is a surprise!

Victoria. Six years, W. O. Six years . . . except to nod to.

43

GANT. Gene, go to the blacksmith and get this chisel sharpened. (EUGENE *exits*.)

VICTORIA. He's a cute one, is that your boy?

GANT. Our youngest.

VICTORIA. All grown up isn't he? Does he get an allowance?

GANT. (*Crossing to her*.) Now, now Victoria, Gene's a good boy, not like his father was.

VICTORIA. Oh, I don't know, I used to think his father was pretty good.

GANT. I was. Wasn't I?

VICTORIA. If you only knew how often the girls and I talk about you all the time up on Eagle Crescent. What gay times we all used to have.

GANT. Life was many songs in those days, Victoria. My dear, dear Victoria—

SONG: *"I CAN'T BELIEVE IT'S YOU"*

LET ME LOOK INTO YOUR EYES
FULL OF WONDER AND SURPRISE
TELL ME HOW YOU KEEP THEM SPARKIN' LIKE
    THEY DO
FATHER TIME HAS LEFT NO TRACE
ETCHED UPON YOUR BABY FACE
I CAN'T BELIEVE IT'S YOU
    VICTORIA.
SEEIN' YOU AGAIN LIKE THIS
MAKES ME WANT TO REMINISCE
    GANT.
YOU ARE TWENTY-ONE AND I AM TWENTY-TWO
    VICTORIA.
I CAN HEAR A BLUEBIRD SING
LIFE IS JUST ETERNAL SPRING
I CAN'T BELIEVE IT'S YOU
    GANT & VICTORIA.
WE COULD HARMONIZE A FAV'RITE OLD
    REFRAIN
LET A MELODY INSPIRE
SOME OF THAT OL' SMOKE AND FIRE
TAKE ME BACK TO YESTERDAY
WHEN THE WORLD WAS YOUNG AND GAY

WHEN WE THOUGHT THE DREAMS WE
    DREAMED WOULD ALL COME TRUE
AM I SLEEPIN' OR AWAKE
PINCH ME NOW, FOR HEAVEN'S SAKE
I CAN'T BELIEVE IT'S YOU

(*Dance extension.*)

TAKE ME BACK TO YESTERDAY
WHEN THE WORLD WAS YOUNG AND GAY
WHEN WE THOUGHT THE DREAMS WE
    DREAMED WOULD ALL COME TRUE
AM I SLEEPIN' OR AWAKE
PINCH ME NOW FOR HEAVEN'S SAKE
I CAN'T BELIEVE IT'S YOU
I CAN'T BELIEVE IT'S YOU
I CAN'T BELIEVE IT'S YOU

VICTORIA. Oh, W. O., W. O.! We do miss you. Time what a thief you are.

GANT. Time hasn't stolen from you. You're still as lovely and stylish as ever. How are all the girls, Victoria?

VICTORIA. (*Crossing Right. Distressed.*) That's what I came to see you about. I lost one of them last night.

GANT. Oh, I'm sorry to hear that.

VICTORIA. Sick only three days. I'd have done anything in the world for her. Even a doctor. I did have two nurses with her night and day.

GANT. Too bad. Too bad. Which one was it?

VICTORIA. Since your time, W. O. We called her Lily.

GANT. Lily?

VICTORIA. Yes, Lily, I couldn't have loved her more if she had been my own daughter. Twenty-two. A child, a mere child, and with such a bright future. No one knows how much I'll miss that girl.

GANT. There! There! I suppose you'll be wanting something for her grave. Here's a sweet lamb—couchant lamb, it's called. "Couchant" means lying down in French. That should be appropriate.

VICTORIA. No, I've already made up my mind—I want that angel. (*Crosses to Carrara angel.*)

GANT. You don't want her, Victoria. Why, she's a white elephant. Nobody can afford to buy her!

VICTORIA. I can and I want her.

GANT. My dear Victoria, I have other fine angels, what about this one? My own carving. We'll put a memorial poem on the base.

To Lily

"She went away in beauty's flower,
Before her youth was spent;
Ere life and love had lived their hour,
God called her—and she went."

VICTORIA. No, ever since I first saw *that* angel, I thought when someone who means something to me goes, she's going to be on the grave.

GANT. That's angel's not for sale, Victoria.

VICTORIA. Then why should you have her out here?

GANT. The truth is, I've promised her to someone. (EUGENE, *entering, finds himself between them.*)

VICTORIA. I'll buy her from whoever you promised and give them a profit. Cash on the line. Who did you sell it to?

GANT. (*Backing Right.*) How about a nice expensive Egyptian urn? Your beloved Lily would like that.

VICTORIA. Egyptian urns—pee pots! I want that angel!

GANT. It's not for sale. Anything you like—ev'rything you like—I'll give it to you—I'll make you a present, for old time's sake. But not my angel.

VICTORIA. Now let's not waste any more time over this. How much, W. O.?

GANT. She's Carrara marble from Italy, and too good for any whore!

VICTORIA. Why you old—

GANT. (*Interrupts.*) Gene, would you please be so kind as to wait upon the madame? (*He escapes to office.*)

VICTORIA. I've heard the trouble your mother's having with that stubborn old mule. Now I believe it.

GENE. Madame Victoria, I believe Papa is saving that angel for his own grave.

VICTORIA. Why didn't he say so? Why didn't he tell me? Poor, poor W. O. Well in that case, when the little lamb is ready, have him send it over—or you bring it over yourself. (VICTORIA *exits.*)

GANT. (*Re-enters.*) When I was a boy your age, I happened to pass a shop something like this. And this very angel was there. And as I looked at her smiling face, I felt more than anything in the world that I wanted to carve delicately with a chisel. It was as though, if I could do that, I could bring something of me out onto a piece of marble. I apprenticed to that stonecutter for five years, and when I left I bought the angel. She's hardly been out of my sight ever since. I bet I've started twenty pieces of marble, but I've never been able to capture her . . . I guess there's no use trying any more—

LAURA. (*Entering with picnic basket.*) Hello, Gene.

EUGENE. Laura.

LAURA. Hello, Mr. Gant.

GANT. Hello!

LAURA. So this is your shop, Mr. Gant.

GANT. This is a real pleasure. Haven't you got fed up with our little resort, young lady?

LAURA. I'm really just beginning to enjoy it here.

GANT. What do you find to enjoy about it?

LAURA. Oh, the countryside is beautiful. Gene and I have had lots of pleasant walks in the hills.

GANT. Oh, so it's Gene who makes it pleasant for you, hey?

EUGENE. Come on, Papa! Hah, hah—

GANT. You're very fond of Gene, aren't you?

LAURA. He's very nice and intelligent.

GANT. Gene's a good boy—our best. Gene, why don't you show Miss James the shop? I'll go sharpen this chisel. (GANT *exits. Pause. He stares and smiles at her.*)

LAURA. I'm afraid I'm bothering you at your work.

EUGENE. Why do you think you might be bothering me?

LAURA. You are supposed to be working.

EUGENE. You came here to see me. What's happened, Laura? Something's different today.

LAURA. (*Crossing Right.*) Oh, don't pay any attention to me. I just—don't know.

EUGENE. What's in the basket?

LAURA. Helen packed us a picnic lunch.

EUGENE. Good! Let's go!

LAURA. Not now.

EUGENE. What is it, Laura? What's the matter? Have I done something wrong?

LAURA. Gene, Helen knows about us! And your father too. He—

EUGENE. I don't care—I want the whole world to know. Here, let's go.

LAURA. (*Sitting on step.*) No. Oh, Gene, I'm so ashamed.

EUGENE. (*Kneeling beside her.*) Laura, my darling, what is it?

LAURA. Gene, I lied to you—I'm twenty-three years old.

EUGENE. Is that all?

LAURA. You're not nineteen either. You're seventeen.

EUGENE. I'm a thousand years old, all the love I've stored up for you.

LAURA. I'm an older woman—

EUGENE. In God's name, what does that have to do with us?

LAURA. There have to be rules!

EUGENE. Rules are made by jealous people. They make rules to love by so even those with no talent for it can at least pretend. We don't need rules. We don't have to pretend. (*MUSIC CUE.*) Oh, Laura, my sweet, what we have is so beautiful, so rare . . . how often in life can you find it?

SONG: *"FEELIN' LOVED"*

NOWHERE DO I SEE
CAUSE FOR BEIN' GLUM
WHAT CAN COME ALONG
WE CAN'T OVERCOME?

I'M A FORTRESS WALL
MADE OF STONE AND VERY TALL
I AM NOT ABOUT TO FALL
I'M FEELIN' LOVED
FEELIN' LOVED ˙
I'M FEELIN' LOVED
FEELIN' LOVED
I'M FEELIN' LOVED
    LAURA.
I'M A HAPPY SMILE
GETTIN' WIDER ALL THE WHILE
OPTIMISTIC BY A MILE
I'M FEELIN' LOVED
FEELIN' LOVED
I'M FEELIN' LOVED
FEELIN' LOVED
I'M FEELIN' LOVED

EUGENE.
SADNESS YOU'RE A STAR
FADING IN THE SKY,
RUNNING FROM THE BREAK OF DAY
   LAURA.
GLADNESS YOU'RE THE SUN
JUST ABOUT TO SHINE
   EUGENE & LAURA.
AND YOUR DAY WILL BE MY LIFETIME

I'M A WISHIN' WELL
UNDERNEATH A MAGIC SPELL
I CAN ONLY WISH YOU WELL
   LAURA.
I'M FEELIN' LOVED
   EUGENE.
FEELIN' LOVED, I'M
   EUGENE & LAURA.
FEELIN' LOVED
FEELIN' LOVED
I'M FEELIN' LOVED
FEELIN' LOVED
I'M FEELIN' LOVED
FEELIN' LOVED
I'M FEELIN' LOVED

(THEY *kiss.* ELIZA *and* WILL *enter.*)

ELIZA. Will, go and tell Mr. Gant that we are here. Hello, Gene. Hello, Miss James. Oh, Miss James, it's five minutes to dinner time at Dixieland, and you know the rules about being late.

EUGENE. Laura and I are going on a picnic.

ELIZA. Not now, you're not. (*To* LAURA.) My dear, I want to talk privately to Mr. Gant—to Eugene, too. I've asked Ben to join us.

EUGENE. We've made plans, Mama.

ELIZA. Son, this is a family conference.

LAURA. Gene, please—I'll wait for you over at Woodruff's. Please. (LAURA *exits.* WILL *enters, then* BEN.)

ELIZA. Is he in there?

WILL. (*Returning from office.*) He's there. We've got him cornered. (BEN *enters.*)

BEN. (*Crossing Right.*) Hello, Uncle Will. Hello, Mama—you look like you just swallowed fifty or a hundred acres. What did you buy today?

ELIZA. Now, Ben, it just so happens that today we are selling. (BEN *sits at work table.* EUGENE *joins him.* GANT *enters wearing coat, tie, and jacket.*)

GANT. Good morning, Miss Eliza.

ELIZA. My, how elegant! Aren't we burning a river this morning?

GANT. I heard you out here, Miss Eliza. I so seldom have a visit from you!

ELIZA. That's most gracious. Well, are we all here? Gene, Ben, Will, Mr. Ga . . .

GANT. This isn't one of your temperance meetings?

ELIZA. (*Ignoring the remark.*) Now, Gene, you want to go to college, don't you?

EUGENE. Very much.

ELIZA. Well, I figure that four years at Chapel Hill will cost thirty-four hundred dollars—but of course you'll have to wait on tables. Otherwise it would be forty-four hundred dollars, which is ridiculous—at the moment we don't even have thirty-four hundred dollars—

GANT. Oh, for God's sake, get to the point, Miss Eliza. Have you got the papers from the bank?

ELIZA. Why what do you mean, what papers?

GANT. You know what I mean. Fish for them, woman! Go ahead, fish for them. (*She turns her back and from her bosom fishes out a large envelope.* GANT *and* EUGENE *laugh.*)

ELIZA. What in the world are you two hyenas laughing at?

GANT. (*Roaring bitter laughing.*) Oh, as you would say, Miss Eliza, that's a good one, that's a good one.

ELIZA. Well, I am glad to see you in a good mood.

GANT. So the bank wants this little old lot, here? That's what you told me, didn't you? Let me see the check.

ELIZA. (*Takes check from envelope, hands it to him.*) Well, it's for twenty thousand dollars. Did you ever see anything like it? Two, zero, comma, zero—zero—zero—decimal—zero —zero!

GANT. "W.O. Gant." It seems to be in good order, all right.

ELIZA. Well—it is—and Will's looked over this deed, and

it's all in order too, isn't it, Will? (*Hands deed to* GANT.)
Give me your pen, Will.

EUGENE. (*Crossing to* GANT.) Papa—the years you've spent
here—all your fine work. Please don't give it up.

ELIZA. Now, Gene, your father knows what he's doing.

EUGENE. But he's such a fine stonecutter.

GANT. You think my work is fine, son? (*Looks about yard.*)

EUGENE. (*Crossing Right to* BEN.) Isn't it, Ben?

ELIZA. (*Between* EUGENE *and* GANT.) Your father knows his
duty to all of us—and to himself—

EUGENE. (*Crossing in to* ELIZA.) You can always recognize
his work. Clean and pure and beautiful. Why should he give
it up? Papa, please don't do it.

BEN. What do you want to do to him, Mama? (GANT *signs
deed.*)

ELIZA. Thank you, Mr. Gant. Now the check. You know
what I'm going to do? I'm going to plan a great, glorious cele-
bration. (*Sees* GANT *looking at check.*) Turn it over, Mr. Gant.
Sign it on the back.

GANT. Why do I have to sign it?

ELIZA. Endorse it. W.O. Gant. You sign it—I'll deposit it
in the Dixieland account, then we draw checks on it.

GANT. We?

ELIZA. Yes. You draw what you want. I'll draw what we
need for Gene's college—for Dixieland, and for anything else
we need.

GANT. I think I'll wait to cash it until I get to Chapel Hill.
The bank has a branch there, doesn't it, Will? (*Gives* WILL
his pen.)

ELIZA. Why would you want to cash it in Chapel Hill?

GANT. This is my check, isn't it? I'm the one who had the
foresight to buy this little pie cornered lot thirty-two years
ago for four hundred dollars—

ELIZA. Now, Mr. Gant, if you're thinking to get my dander
up!

GANT. Miss Eliza, I've been wanting to get away from here
for a long time. I'm taking Gene with me. (*Crosses to* EUGENE.)
I'm going to put him in that college there at Chapel Hill.

EUGENE. Now?

GANT. Now! And then I'm going to travel—and when Gene's
free in the summer, we'll travel together. (*Crosses back to*
ELIZA.) And I can just see the word Dixieland forming on

your cursed lips. What about Dixieland? Nothing for Dixieland? *No,* not one God-damn red cent! You've plenty of property of your own you can sell. If it's rest and comfort you really want, sell it, woman, sell it! (*Puts check in pocket. Crosses to* BEN.) Goodbye, Ben. Tell Helen—tell Helen I'll write. So long, dear Carrara angel. I'll arrange for us to be together again some day. C'mon, Gene. (*Heads for the door.*)

ELIZA. (*Leaping at* GANT.) I won't let you do this. I won't let you. (*Seizing check from his pocket, tears check.*)

EUGENE. *Mama!*

ELIZA. All right, all right, all right! There's your check. I'm going to put an injunction against you. I'll prove you're not responsible to sell this property, or even to own it. I'll get guardianship over you! Everyone knows the times you've been to the cure—the threats you've made to me—you're a madman, Mr. Gant, a madman. I'll fight you tooth and nail, tooth and nail. And I'll win.

GANT. All those things you said about me are true. Why don't you let me go?

ELIZA. Because you're my husband. We must try to understand and love each other. We must try. (*Exits.* WILL *follows her.*)

GANT. (*Quietly.*) Eugene, go over to Laughran's and get me a bottle. You heard me.

EUGENE. No, Papa.

GANT. Are you still paddling along after your mother?

BEN. Leave Gene alone. If you want to get sick, do it yourself.

GANT. Ungrateful sons! Oh, the sad waste of years, the red wound of all our mistakes. (*Exits.* EUGENE *looks after him.*)

BEN. The fallen Titan. He might have made it if he hadn't tried to take you. He could still make it, but he won't try again.

EUGENE. They loved each other once. They must have had one moment in time that was perfect. What happened? It frightens me, Ben; how can something so perfect turn into this torture?

BEN. They're strangers. They don't know each other. No one ever really comes to know anyone.

EUGENE. That's not true. I know you—I know Laura.

BEN. Listen to him! No matter what arms may clasp us, what heart may warm us, what mouth may kiss us, we remain strangers. We never escape it. Never, never, never. (*Closes eyes. Leans back.*)

EUGENE. Ben! Hey, Ben? Ben, you're burning up! Come on —put your arms around me. I'm going to take you home.

BEN. (*Breaking away Left.*) Can't. It's all right, I'm just tired.

EUGENE. Why didn't you tell somebody you're sick, you crazy idiot! (*Running to entrance.*) Papa! Papa!

BEN. (*Crossing down steps, then sits on stoop.*) To hell with them, Gene. To hell with them all. Don't give a damn for anything. Nothing gives a damn for you. There are a lot of bad days, there are a lot of good ones—that's all there is . . . a lot of days . . . My God, is there no freedom on this earth? (GANT *enters.*)

EUGENE. (*Supporting* BEN.) Papa, Ben's sick. He's burning up. I'm taking him home. Call Dr. Maguire. (EUGENE *exits with* BEN. GANT *at phone.*)

GANT. Hello, Dottie. Get me Dr. Maguire. Get him over to my house right away. It's my son, Ben. (*To Carrara angel.*) And still you smile . . .

FADE OUT

ACT TWO

SCENE 2

SCENE: *The Boarding House, that evening.* MAGUIRE *and* HELEN *are hovering over* BEN *on the parlor couch.* FATTY *waits in the dining room.* ELIZA *on veranda bench,* LAURA *on swing,* GANT *crossing Right to rocker, sits.*

EUGENE. (*Crosses to* ELIZA.) Mama, when can I see Ben?

ELIZA. When the doctor says. I'll tell you what: when you do, don't make out like Ben is sick. Just make a big joke of it—laugh as big as you please—

EUGENE. (*Sits on porch steps.*) Mama!

ELIZA. Well, it's the sick one's frame of mind that counts. I remember when I was teaching school in Hominy township, I had pneumonia. Nobody expected me to live, but I—did— I got through it somehow. I remember one day I was sitting down—I reckon I was convalescing. Old Doc Fletcher had been there—and as he left I saw him shake his head at my cousin Sally. "Why, Eliza, what on earth," she says, just as soon as he had gone, "he tells me you're spitting up blood every time you cough: you've got consumption as sure as you live!" "Pshaw!" I said. I remember I was just determined to make a big joke of it. "I don't believe a word of it," I said. "Not one single word." And it was because I didn't believe it that *I got well.*

GANT. (*Quietly.*) Eliza, don't run on so.

HELEN. (*Comes out of house.*) The doctor says Mama can seen Ben, but no one else yet.

EUGENE. How is he?

HELEN. (*Crossing for* ELIZA, *takes her to* BEN.) You know Dr. Maguire. If you can get anything out of him . . .

GANT. (*Moans worriedly.*) Oh God, I don't like the feel of it. I don't like the feel of it.

BEN. (*Weakly.*) Maguire, if you don't stop hanging over me I'll smother to death.

HELEN. (*Following* ELIZA.) Mama's here, Ben.

ELIZA. (*Speaking as though to a baby.*) Why hello, son— did you think I wasn't ever coming to see you?

HELEN. (*After a pause.*) Ben, Mama's here.

ELIZA. (*To* MAGUIRE.) Can't he talk? Why doesn't he look at me?

DR. MAGUIRE. (*Head of couch.*) Ben, you can hear what they're saying, can't you?

BEN. (*Quietly, his eyes still closed.*) I wish you'd all get out and leave me alone.

ELIZA. What kind of talk is that? You have to be looked after, son!

BEN. Then let Mrs. Pert look after me.

HELEN. Ben!

BEN. Maguire, where's Fatty? I want to see Fatty.

HELEN. Ben, how can you talk that way? If it weren't for that woman you wouldn't be sick now. Drinking, carousing with her night after night—

BEN. (*Yells with dwindling strength.*) Fatty! (MRS. PERT starts towards BEN.)

HELEN. (*To* BEN.) You ought to be ashamed!

DR. MAGUIRE. Mrs. Gant, we need some more cold cloths. Why don't you—

HELEN. (*Crosses angrily to* MAGUIRE.) Do you have to add

to her misery? When you need something, ask me. They're in the kitchen. (ELIZA *and* HELEN *cross to veranda.*)

DR. MAGUIRE. It's all right, Mrs. Pert. Ben seems to want you here. (HE *exits.* FATTY *goes to* BEN.)

BEN. (*Immediately turns toward her.*) Fatty?

EUGENE. How does he seem, Mama?

ELIZA. (*Crossing with* HELEN *to bench.*) He couldn't stand to see me worrying. (*They sit.*)

EUGENE. I remember the early mornings when Ben and I used to take the paper route together. Ben used to make up stories for me about all the sleeping people in all the sleeping houses! He always used to throw the papers as lightly as he could because he hated to wake them. I remember.

GANT. (*Groaning.*) Oh Jesus, it's fearful—that this should be put on me, old and sick as I am—

HELEN. (*In blazing fury. Crosses to him.*) You shut your mouth this minute, you damned old man! I've spent my life taking care of you! Everything's been done for you—everything—and you'll be here when we're all gone—so don't let us hear anything about your sickness, you selfish old man—it makes me furious!

GANT. (*Rises and slowly crosses Left, down steps to swing area.*) When the old die, no one cares. But the young . . . the young . . .

EUGENE. I would care, Papa.

DR. MAGUIRE. (*At front door.*) If any of you are interested, Ben is a little better.

EUGENE. Thank God!

HELEN. Ben is better? Why didn't you say so before?

ELIZA. I could have told you! I could have told you! I had a feeling all along!

GANT. Well! We can all relax now.

DR. MAGUIRE. (*Crossing Left.*) I'll be back in a little while. (*Motions* GANT *away from the others.*) Gant, it's both lungs now. I can't tell them. But see to it that they stay around. I'm going next door and phone for some oxygen. It may ease it a little for him. It won't be long. (*He gives* GANT *a fond, strengthening touch, exits. MUSIC CUE.*)

BEN. Fatty? Fatty, stay with me.

FATTY. Hush, Ben. Be quiet, dear. Save yourself.

BEN. Hold my hand, Fatty. Sing to me. It's one way to step out of a photograph, isn't it? (GANT *sits on swing.*)

SONG: *"A MEDLEY"*

FATTY.
YOU'RE GONNA DRIFT ON A SUMMER BREEZE
OVER TREES
'CROSS THE SEAS
BEN.
PICTURE MYSELF WITH AN EAGLE'S EYE
WITH BRIGHT FEATHERED WINGS I WILL FLY
FATTY.
AND FLY LIKE THE EAGLES
WAY UP . . .
(BEN *dies.*)
FATTY. (*At front door.*) Ben's gone. (EUGENE *up, crosses Left.*)
ELIZA.
EV'RY SOUL A SAILOR
SAILING OUT TO SEA
DRIFTING, DRIFTING
NESTLED CLOSE TOGETHER
SAFELY AT THE START
THEN DRIFTING DRIFTING
    APART
LAURA.
WHERE CAN HE TURN FOR
    COMFORT BUT ME
SO LET ME COMFORT HIM NOW

LET IT BE A LOVE OF JOY OR SORROW
LET IT BE TONIGHT AND NOT TOMORROW
SURELY AS HE NEEDS ME
I WON'T BACK AWAY
IF I EVER LOVED HIM
COULD I EVER LOVE HIM (*Crosses to* EUGENE.)
MORE THAN I LOVE HIM TODAY?
MORE THAN I LOVE HIM TODAY?

FADE OUT

ACT TWO

SCENE 3

SCENE: *The Dixieland Boarding House, before dawn, two weeks later. GANT is seated on the veranda steps, empty whiskey bottle in hand. He is quiet and reflective.*

SONG: *"TOMORROW I'M GONNA BE OLD"*

GANT.
IF TIME WERE MONEY
THERE WAS A TIME
I WAS A MILLIONAIRE
ROLLIN' IN MINUTES AND HOURS
WITH YEAR UPON YEAR TO SPARE
IT NEVER CROSSED MY MIND
IT NEVER CROSSED MY MIND
HOW MUCH TIME A FELLA HAS
TILL A FELLA HAS NO MORE TIME

SHINE UP THE MOON AND THE
    STARS IN THE SKY
AND LET THE GOOD TIMES ROLL
TONIGHT I'M A CHILD
I'M CAREFREE AND WILD
TOMORROW I'M GONNA BE OLD

ROLL OUT A DREAM AND I'LL
    MAKE IT COME TRUE
I GOT A MAGIC SOUL
TONIGHT I'M A WINNER
A NAIEVE BEGINNER
TOMORROW I'M GONNA BE OLD

TONIGHT I'M A HERO
I CAN AND I WILL, YES
IT'S RAINING BUT I SEE THE SUN
MY HOPES ARE OUTRAGEOUS
BUT I AM COURAGEOUS
AND NOTHIN' AND NO ONE WILL SEE ME
    UNDONE, SO

BRING ON A RAVISHING
    BLONDE OR BRUNETTE
AND LET ME LOSE CONTROL
TONIGHT I DELIGHT IN
WHATEVER'S EXCITIN'
TOMORROW I'M GONNA BE—
    MAYBE JUST POSSIBLY—
TOMORROW I'M GONNA BE—
    NOT THAT I WANNA BE—
TOMORROW I'M GONNA BE OLD

(*Dance extension.*)

SO BRING ON A RAVISHING
    BLONDE OR BRUNETTE
AND LET ME LOSE CONTROL
TONIGHT I DELIGHT IN
WHATEVER'S EXCITIN'
TOMORROW I'M GONNA BE—
    MAYBE JUST POSSIBLY—
TOMORROW I'M GONNA BE—
NOT THAT I WANNA BE
TOMORROW I'M GONNA BE—

IF TIME WERE MONEY
THERE WAS A TIME
I WAS A MILLIONAIRE
ROLLIN' IN MINUTES AND HOURS
WITH YEAR UPON YEAR TO SPARE
IT NEVER CROSSED MY MIND
HOW MUCH TIME A FELLA HAS
IT NEVER CROSSED MY MIND.

(GANT *exits into house. The House Unit revolves to POSI-TION #5 revealing dining and* LAURA'S *room.* LAURA *is in bed.* EUGENE *is at the foot of the bed by the window putting on his shirt.*)

    LAURA. (*Stirring.*) Gene?
    EUGENE. It's getting light, it's nearly dawn.
    LAURA. Don't go yet.
    EUGENE. Do you think I want to on your last morning here?

Mama gets up so early. Do you know that every morning before she cooks breakfast she visits Ben's grave?

LAURA. (*They kiss.*) Gene, Gene.

EUGENE. Oh Laura, I love you so. When I'm close to you like this, it's so natural. Are all men like me? Tell me.

LAURA. I've told you I've never known anyone like you.

EUGENE. But you have known men? It would seem strange if you hadn't. A woman so beautiful, so loving. You make me feel like I only used to dream of feeling. I've hardly thought to daydream in weeks—except about us.

LAURA. What did you used to dream?

EUGENE. I always wanted to be the winner, the general, the spearhead of victory! Then following that I wanted to be loved. Victory and love! Unbeaten and beloved. And I am that now, truly! Laura, will you marry me? You knew I was going to ask you, didn't you? You knew I couldn't let you go even for a day.

LAURA. (*Crossing away.*) Yes, I knew.

EUGENE. (*Crossing to her, embrace.*) You're happy with me. You know I make you happy. And I'm so complete with you. Do you know that three hundred dollars Ben left me? He would want me to use it for us. I'll go with you to Richmond today. I'll meet your parents, so they won't think I'm an irresponsible fool who's stolen you. It may be a little hard to prove—but there is a job I can get. Would you mind living in Altamont?

LAURA. I don't care where I live. Just keep holding me. (*MUSIC CUE.*)

EUGENE. I am going to have to tell Mama first.

LAURA. Never mind about that. Tell me about us.

SONG: *"FEELIN' LOVED"* (REPRISE)

EUGENE.
SADNESS YOU'RE A STAR
    FADING IN THE SKY
RUNNING FROM THE BREAK OF DAY
    LAURA.
GLADNESS YOU'RE THE SUN
    JUST ABOUT TO SHINE
EUGENE & LAURA.
AND YOUR DAY WILL BE MY LIFETIME

I'M A WISHIN' WELL
UNDERNEATH A MAGIC SPELL
I CAN ONLY WISH YOU WELL
I'M FEELIN' LOVED
FEELIN' LOVED
I'M FEELIN' LOVED
FEELIN' LOVED
I'M FEELIN' LOVED
FEELIN' LOVED
I'M FEELIN' LOVED

(*From a far distance, they hear the whistle of a train as it passes.*)

EUGENE. The Richmond train leaves at noon. I'll have to get packed.
LAURA. You do love trains, don't you?
EUGENE. I love only you. Will you have confidence in me, the unbeaten and beloved?
LAURA. Yes, darling, I will have confidence in you.
EUGENE. I will never have to sneak out of this room again. (EUGENE *starts for the door.*)
LAURA. Eugene! I will love you always. (EUGENE *exits.*)

SONG: *"HOW DO YOU SAY GOODBYE"*

HOW DO YOU SAY GOODBYE
WHEN IT IS TIME TO SAY IT
AND YOU DON'T WANT TO SAY IT
HOW DO YOU EVEN TRY

THERE ARE NO EARTHLY WORDS
    GENTLE ENOUGH FOR HEALING
ONE BROKEN HEARTED FEELING
HOW DO YOU SAY GOODBYE

HOW COULD I SAY I'M SORRY
FOR FALLING IN LOVE WITH YOU
WHAT'S TO BE GAINED REGRETTING
A LOVE THAT WAS SWEET AND TRUE

BETTER TO TURN AWAY
NEVER TO SAY IT'S OVER

THOUGH I COULD SAY IT'S OVER
IT WOULD BE JUST A LIE
LOVE DOESN'T SIMPLY DIE
HOW DO YOU SAY GOODBYE

HOW COULD I SAY I'M SORRY
FOR FALLING IN LOVE WITH YOU
WHAT'S TO BE GAINED REGRETTING
A LOVE THAT WAS SWEET AND TRUE

BETTER TO TURN AWAY
NEVER TO SAY IT'S OVER
THOUGH I COULD SAY IT'S OVER
IT WOULD BE JUST A LIE
LOVE DOESN'T SIMPLY DIE
HOW DO YOU SAY GOODBYE.

(*The dinning room.* EUGENE *at the telephone doesn't see* ELIZA *returning to the house.*)

EUGENE. Good morning. Three-two, please— Hello, Uncle Will? This is Eugene— Yes, I know how early it is— You know that position you offered me? I've decided to take it. (ELIZA *at the door, pleased.*) I've thought it over and that's what I'd like to do, for a while anyway— That's right—that's fine— Well, you see, I'm getting married—yes, married—to Miss James. We're leaving on the noon train—thanks, Uncle Will. Thanks a lot. (*Hangs up phone.*)

ELIZA. (*Entering dining room.*) Eugene!

EUGENE. Well, now—with your second sense, I thought you would have guessed it, Mama.

ELIZA. Why didn't I know, why didn't I see?

EUGENE. I'm sorry, Mama, but we couldn't wait any longer.

ELIZA. Gene, child, don't make this mistake. She's so much older than you. Don't throw yourself away, boy!

EUGENE. Mama, there's no use arguing. Nothing you can say will change my mind.

ELIZA. (*Desperately.*) And my plans for you? What of my plans for you?

EUGENE. Mama, I don't want your plans, I've got my own life to live! (*Starts for the door,* ELIZA *follows.*)

ELIZA. But you don't know! Gene, listen, you know that

Stumptown property of mine? I sold it just yesterday so you could go to Chapel Hill— You know I've always wanted you to have an education. You can have it now, child, you can have it.

EUGENE. It's too late, Mama, it's too late!

ELIZA. Why pshaw, child, it's never too late for anything! It's what Ben wanted, you know.

EUGENE. Laura and I are leaving, Mama. I'm going up to get packed. (*Exits.*)

ELIZA. Gene! (ELIZA *stands looking after him a moment, then quickly lifts the telephone receiver.*) Three-two, please. (*Waits.*)

HELEN. (*Enters from kitchen, with a broom with which she sweeps the hallway.*) What are you calling Uncle Will so early for?

ELIZA. (*Into phone.*) Will? No, no, I know—I heard— Yes, I know it's early— Listen, Will, I want you to do something for me. You know my Stumptown property? I want you to sell it— Now, this morning— Will, don't argue with me— I don't care what it's worth. Call Cash Rankin, he's been after me for weeks to sell— Well, I know what I want to do— I'll explain it to you later— Just do what I say and let me know. (*She hangs up.*)

HELEN. Well, it's never too early in the morning to turn trade, is it? What are you selling?

ELIZA. Some property I own. Helen, get breakfast started, will you? I'll be in later. There's something I have to take care of. And if Gene comes down, keep him in there, will you?

HELEN. Oh, all right. You let me know when I can let him out! (ELIZA *crosses up the stairs to* LAURA's *room.* HELEN *disappears into the kitchen. Lights are up in* LAURA's *room. She is sitting, writing a letter.* ELIZA *appears at door of* LAURA's *room.*)

LAURA. Oh, Mrs. Gant. I've been expecting you. (*As* ELIZA *enters.*)

ELIZA. I should think you would.

LAURA. Mrs. Gant, before you say anything—

ELIZA. I'll vow I can't believe a mature woman would take advantage of a child, a mere child—

LAURA. Mrs. Gant, will you please listen?

ELIZA. (*Tossing her nightgown from head of bed into suitcase.*) I will listen to nothing. You just pack your things and get out of this house. I should have known what you were from the first minute I set eyes on you . . . "I'm looking for a room, Mrs. Gant . . ." Why butter wouldn't melt in your mouth—

LAURA. (*Slowly, distinctly.*) Mrs. Gant, I am not marrying Eugene. I'm not. I wish with all my heart I could! (*Crossing to head of bed, the women counter each other.*)

ELIZA. You can't lie out of it. Gene just told me.

LAURA. I am engaged to be married to a young man in Richmond.

ELIZA. What kind of a wicked game are you playing with my child?

LAURA. I know I should have told Gene long ago—but I didn't. A girl about to get married suddenly finds herself facing responsibilities. I never liked (ELIZA *sits at vanity.*) responsibilities. Gene knows how I am. I like music, I like to walk in the woods, I like—to dream. I know I'm older than Gene, but in many ways I'm younger. The thought of marriage frightened me. I told my fiance I needed time to think it over. I fell in love with Eugene. I found the kind of romance I'd never known before, but I've also found that it isn't the answer. Gene is a wonderful boy, Mrs. Gant. He must go to college. He must have room to expand and grow, to find himself. He mustn't be tied down at this point in his life. He needs the whole world to wander in—and I know now that I need a home, I need children—I need a husband. For people like me there are rules, very good rules for marriage and for happiness—and I've broken enough of them. I telephoned Philip last night. He's arriving at the depot on that early train. We're going on to Charleston together, and we'll be married there. He loves me, and I will love him too after a while. (*Takes note.*) I left this note for Eugene. I couldn't just tell him. (*Gives it to* ELIZA. *Crosses for bag.*) Will you say goodbye to Mr. Gant for me, and tell him I hope he feels better? And my goodbyes to Mr. Clatt and the others? And to Helen. Especially to Helen. She works so hard. (*Picks up suitcase, faces* ELIZA.) Someday you're going to have to let him go, too. Goodbye, Mrs. Gant. (*She exits room crossing downstairs and off Left.*)

EUGENE. (*Entering* LAURA's *room.*) Laura? Laura? (*Enters, to* ELIZA.) Mama! Where's Laura?

ELIZA. She's gone.

EUGENE. Gone? Where?

ELIZA. She had to go. She left.

EUGENE. You sent her away.

ELIZA. I never did. She just walked out on you, child.

EUGENE. Laura!

ELIZA. (EUGENE *breaks for the door.* ELIZA *picks up the letter, runs after him.*) Gene! Eugene! Wait! (*House Unit revolves to POSITION #1.*)

EUGENE. (*Runs down to veranda.*) Laura—Laura—Laura—

ELIZA. Wait! Wait! She left you this. Gene! She left you this letter. Read it, child. (EUGENE *takes the letter and reads it while sitting on the swing.* HELEN *enters.*)

HELEN. Mama, we've got to start getting breakfast.

LAURA'S VOICE.
HOW COULD I SAY I'M
    SORRY

(ELIZA *waves her to silence.*)

ELIZA. That Miss James. She and Eugene.

FOR FALLING IN LOVE
    WITH YOU

HELEN. Oh, my God, Mama, have you just found out about that? What about it?

WHAT'S TO BE
    GAINED REGRET-
    TING

ELIZA. She's gone.

HELEN. What?

LAURA'S VOICE.
A LOVE THAT WAS
    SWEET AND TRUE

ELIZA. She just walked out on him.

HELEN. Oh, so that's it, is it? Has your girl gone and left you, huh? Why, Gene, forget about it! She's a grown woman.

BETTER TO TURN
    AWAY

ELIZA. Helen's right. Why, child, I wouldn't let a girl get the best of me. She was just fooling you all the time, wasn't she, Helen?

NEVER TO SAY IT'S
    OVER

HELEN. You'll forget her in a week, Gene.

ELIZA. Why, of course you will. Pshaw, this was just puppy love. Like the fellow says, there's plenty good fish in the sea as ever came out of it.

HELEN. Cheer up, you're not the only man got fooled in his life!

ELIZA. Helen, go inside, I'll be in in a minute.

HELEN. Oh, all right. (HELEN exits.)

THOUGH I COULD SAY IT'S OVER

IT WOULD BE JUST A LIE

LOVE DOESN'T SIMPLY DIE

HOW DO YOU SAY GOODBYE

ELIZA. (Sitting Right of EUGENE.) Why, I'd be ashamed to let any girl get my goat like that. When you get older, you'll just look back on this and laugh. You'll see. You'll be going to college next year, and you won't remember a thing about it. I told you I sold my Stumptown property, and I have. This year's term has started already, but next year—

EUGENE. Mama, now! Now! I've wasted enough time!

ELIZA. What are you talking about? Why you're a child yet, there's plenty of time yet—

EUGENE. Mama, Mama, what is it? What more do you want from me? Do you want more string? Do you want me to collect more bottles? Tell me what you want! Do you want more property? Do you want the town? Is that it?

ELIZA. (Crossing Right.) Why, I don't know what you're talking about, boy. If I hadn't tried to accumulate a little something, none of you would have had a roof to call your own.

EUGENE. (Following.) A roof to call our own? Good God, I never had a bed to call my own! I never had a room to call my own! I never had a quilt to call my own that wasn't taken from me to warm the mob that rocks on the porch and grumbles.

ELIZA. Now you may sneer at the boarders if you like.

EUGENE. Ever since I was this high, and you sent me to the store for the groceries, I used to think, "This food is not for us—it's for them!" Mama, making us wait until they've eaten, all these years—feeding us on their leftovers—do you know what that does to us?—when it's you we needed for us. Why? Why?

ELIZA. They don't hurt me like the rest of you do—they wouldn't talk to me like you are, for one thing.

EUGENE. Because they don't care—they're strangers. They don't give a damn about you! They'll talk like this about you behind your back—I've heard them do it plenty! Doesn't it matter to you what I say? (*He embraces her.*)

ELIZA. I don't understand.

EUGENE. (*Releasing her, he moves Left.*) Oh, it's easy to cry now, Mama, but it won't do you any good! I've done as much work for my wages as you deserve. I've given you fair value for your money, I thank you for nothing.

ELIZA. What are you saying?

EUGENE. By God, I shall spend the rest of my life getting my heart back, healing and forgetting every scar you put upon me. The first move I ever made after the cradle was to crawl for the door. And now, at last, I am free. Free from all of you. (*Crosses up steps to front door.*)

ELIZA. Gene! Gene, you're not leaving?

EUGENE. Ah, you were not looking, were you? Mama, I've already gone. (EUGENE *exits into the house.* ELIZA *sits on the veranda steps, stunned.* GANT *enters from the house.*)

GANT. Now do you suppose I can get some breakfast? (ELIZA *doesn't answer.*) Well, do you mind if I make a fire in the fireplace? (*Goes to the wood box, muttering.*) If I can't get any food to keep me alive, I can get a little warmth out of this drafty barn! (*Starts collecting wood from box.*) Some day I'm going to burn up this house—just pile in all the logs that old grate'll hold—and all the furniture—and all the wooden headed people around here—and some kerosene—till this old barn takes off like a giant cinder blazing through the sky. That would show them—all fifteen miserable rooms— burning, blistering—

ELIZA. I wish you would, Mr. Gant. I just wish you would. (*MUSIC CUE.*)

GANT. You think I'm joking.

ELIZA. No, I don't.

GANT. If I just get drunk enough, I will.

ELIZA. (*Rises, faces house.*) Serve it right—miserable, unholy house!

GANT. Why, Miss Eliza!

ELIZA. I'll do it myself— (*With demoniacal strength she shakes porch railing.*) I'll tear you down! I'll kill you, house, kill you! I'll shake you to pieces! (*The railing pulls from porch. They laugh.* GANT *knocks down railing post.*)

GANT. (*Screaming up at house. Brandishing torn pillar.*) Clatt— Mangle— Brown— Come out of there, you rats, all of you—come out, come out, wherever you are! (*The* BOARDERS *begin to yell and squeal from inside.*)

ELIZA. (*Hysterically imitating* GANT, *crossing Left.*) Come out, come out, wherever you are!

HELEN. (*Entering with dinner bell.*) What's going on?

GANT. We're tearing down this murderous trap, that's what. Give me that bell. Hand me the hatchet, it's in the wood box.

ELIZA. Fine! Fine! I'll get it. (*Dashes to wood box, takes out hatchet.* BOARDERS *enter downstairs in various stages of undress.*)

MISS BROWN. Call the police.

MRS. CLATT. Let's go to Mrs. Haskell's!

JAKE. Gant's off his nut!

GANT. (*Chasing them off Left, threatening the* BOARDERS *with dinner bell.*) Squeal, you croaking bastards. Croak and run! Run for your lives!

BOARDERS. (*Ad lib as they scurry off.*)
The house is falling down.
It's a tornado!
Ladies' Temperance Society, humph!
Has anyone called the police?
(*Etc.* ELIZA *and* HELEN *destroy drainpipes, brackets, railings. Finally* ELIZA *attacks the Dixieland sign. It comes crashing to the ground.*)

GANT. Oh, Miss Eliza, what a woman you are.

SONG: *"GANT'S WALTZ"*

SEEIN' YOU BEHAVE THIS WAY
TAKES ME BACK TO YESTERDAY
YOU ARE TWENTY-ONE AND I AM TWENTY-TWO

(*Dance extension.*)

ELIZA. (*Returning to reality.*) Mr. Gant, Mr. Gant, what have you done? What have you done?

GANT. What have I done? What have I— Merciful God, woman!

ELIZA. Just look at this mess! And the boarders have all gone!

HELEN. (*At veranda bench.*) I don't know what got into you, Papa.

GANT. Merciful God! What got into me? Didn't she just stand there herself and—

ELIZA. Helen, go get the boarders, tell them he's been drinking, tell them anything, but get them back!

GANT. (*Holding* HELEN *from going.*) Let them go, Miss Eliza. Let the boarders go! (ELIZA *stands rigid.* GANT *waits anxiously.*)

ELIZA. (*Starts picking up debris.*) I just don't know what came over me.

GANT. (*Releasing* HELEN, *she exits Left.*) Merciful God! (EUGENE *enters with his suitcase.*) Where are *you* going?

EUGENE. I'm going to school at Chapel Hill, Papa.

GANT. You are? (*He looks at* ELIZA.)

EUGENE. Mama promised me the money. She sold her Stumptown property.

GANT. (*Crosses to Right of her.*) Oh? By God, maybe it isn't going to be such a God-damned miserable day, after all! Got any money, son?

EUGENE. I've got Ben's money. Thanks, Papa.

GANT. (*Takes money from his pocket, tucks it into* EUGENE's *pocket.*) Well, go, Gene. Go for both of us. Keep right on going.

EUGENE. I will, Papa. Goodbye.

GANT. Goodbye, Gene. (*Starts into house, turns.*) You're going to bust loose, boy—you're going to bust loose, all over this dreary planet! (GANT *exits thru front door.*)

ELIZA. (*Sweeping.*) I reckon you've made up your mind all right.

EUGENE. Yes, Mama, I have.

ELIZA. Well, I'll deposit the money in the Chapel Hill Bank for you. It seems I've hardly laid eyes on you all summer long— Well, when you get up there, you want to look up your Uncle Emerson and Aunt Lucy. When you're in a strange town it's might good sometimes to have someone you know. You might just tell them not to be surprised to see me anytime now. (*She nods pertly at him.*) I reckon I can pick right up and light out the same as the next fellow when I get ready. I'm not going to spend all my days slaving away for a lot of boarders—it don't pay. (*Her talk drifts off.* EUGENE *stands*

looking at her. There is another terrible silence between them.)
I hate to see you go, son.
EUGENE. Goodbye, Mama.
ELIZA. Try to be happy, child, try to be a little more
happy . . .
EUGENE. (*Rushing to her arms.*) Mama! (*MUSIC CUE.*)
ELIZA. There, there boy, you're gonna be all right. Just fine.
Now don't you worry one single bit— (*Continues song.*)
MAKE A LITTLE SUNSHINE ON SOMEONE
AND FEEL THE SUN SHINE ON YOU
Now for heaven's sake, spruce up, boy, spruce up! Throw your
shoulders back! And smile, look pleasant! Let them know up
there that you are somebody! (EUGENE *starts to leave, stops
when he hears* BEN's *voice.*)

SONG: *"LIKE THE EAGLES FLY"* (REPRISE)

BEN's VOICE.
CLIMBIN' AND DIVIN' AND CIRCLIN' AROUND
FREER THAN FREE YOU'LL BE WAY OFF THE
    GROUND
EUGENE & BEN's VOICE.
SWOOPIN' AND LOOPIN' THE HAPPIEST BIRD
RIDIN' THE CLOUDS LIKE SOME BUFFALO HERD

I'M GONNA SAIL LIKE THE EAGLES SAIL
FEATHERED TAIL
OUT OF JAIL
KISS ALL MY CARES AND MY WOES GOODBYE
    WITH SUN ON MY WINGS, I WILL FLY
        FLY LIKE THE EAGLES FLY
           WAY UP HIGH
BEN's VOICE.
IN THE SKY.

(EUGENE *exits Left as the curtain falls.*)

CURTAIN

PROPERTY PLOT

ON THE VERANDA—
wicker chair
wicker bench
wicker rocker
wicker table with Altamont
    newspaper
breakaways: DIXIELAND sign,
    stoop tops, railings,
    brackets, drainpipe,
    windows

IN THE PARLOR—
piano with sheet music
piano stool
couch
parlor desk with DIXIELAND
    advertising cards on
    top and hand drawn map
    in drawer

IN THE DINING ROOM—
round table with tablecloth
    and four chairs
square table with tablecloth
    and three chairs
sideboard with telephone and
    seven sets of knives,
    forks and spoons*
    dinner bell, playing cards

IN THE KITCHEN—
try with seven glasses*
server with mock fish for
    seven*
charlotte russe and knife*
pitcher with water*
two glasses lemonade
broom

tray with coffee pot and
    service for eight
two towel compresses in
    shallow pan
dinner napkins*

IN THE KEEPING ROOM—
    day bed
    desk with Mrs. Pert's knitting
        basket, Eliza's sewing
        basket on top and bed-
        sheet in drawer
    desk chair

TOP OF STAIRS—
    Mr. Farrel's suitcase

LAURA'S ROOM—
    iron bed with pillow and sheet
    writing desk with paper and pencil
        in drawer
    desk stool
    three-sided folding screen
    dresser

UPPER BACK ROOM—
    small pitcher of water and glass,
        blanket and pillow. These for
        Eliza to carry into the keeping
        room scene in I-2

IN THE YARD—
    tree swing (porch swing variety)
    wicker table and two chairs

STAGE LEFT PROP TABLE—
    Eugene's writing book and pencil
    grocery basket
    real estate circulars
    three geranium flower pots
    Laura's suitcase

*HELEN GANT uses these props to set tables during ALL
THE COMFORTS OF HOME and serve the BOARDERS
dinner during the first section of ACT ONE, Scene one.

Dixieland advertising card
Laura's purse with paper money
    including twenty dollars in
    one dollar bills
Maguire's doctor's bag with stethescope
ukelele
Ben's cigarettes and matches
deed and check
picnic basket
Will's fountain pen
Gant's liquor bottle

RUNNING PLOT

During the Keeping Room scene in I-2;

Set—
    beer bottles around veranda
    two full beer bottles by bench
    two glasses by bench
    ukelele on bench
    garbage pail by side door

Strike—
    Laura's hat

Act Two Preset—

Set—
marble yard props and hanging pieces
Strike—
    everything from kitchen except
    broom (from swing area) dinner
        bell, compresses and pan
    beer bottles from porch
    lemonade glasses from swing area

Preset behind Marble Yard for II-2;

Set—
    blanket and pillow on parlor couch
    Maguire's bag by couch
    piano stool by couch
    wood box by side door

Laura's packing clothes behind folding screen
paper and pencil on Laura's writing desk
Laura's costume change behind folding screen

End of II-1
Strike—
   marble yard

End of II-2
Strike—
   pillow, blanket, compresses
   and pan from couch area
   piano stool back to piano

Stage Right Prop Table—
   trowel
   water can
   beer bottles
   wood box with wood and hatchet

In the Marble Yard—
   work table with marble slab, hammer and chisel
   pushbroom
   sand barrel
   Egyptian urn
   couchant lamb
   angel
   Carrara angel
   telephone

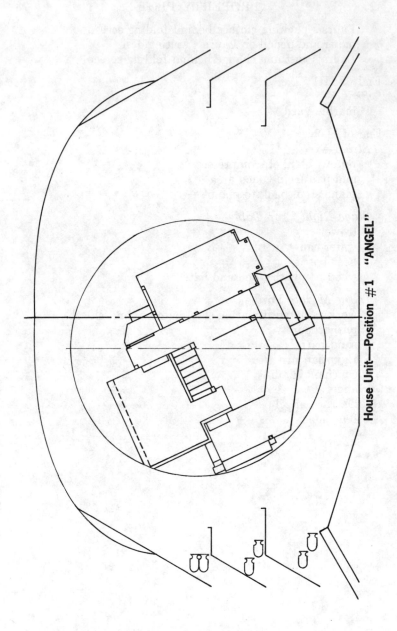

House Unit—Position #1 "ANGEL"

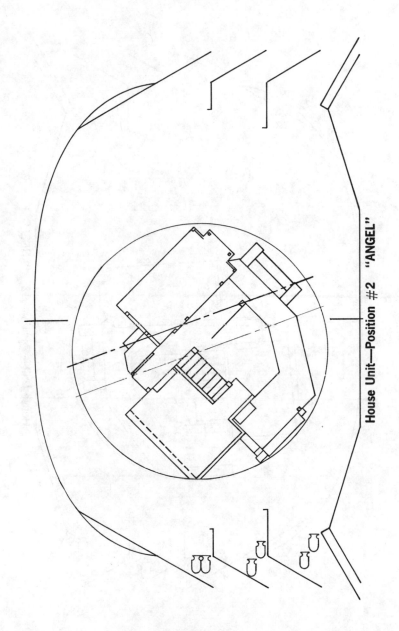

House Unit—Position #2 "ANGEL"

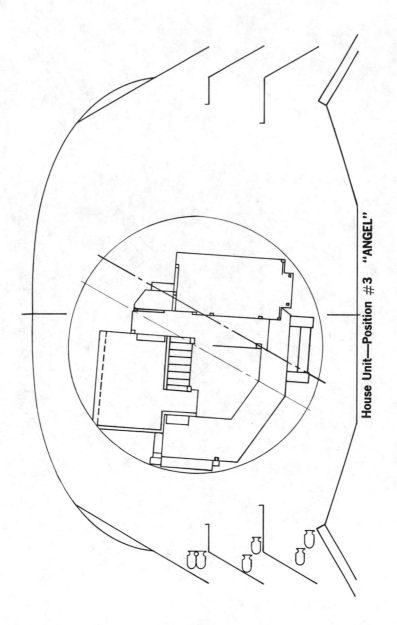

House Unit—Position #3 "ANGEL"

76

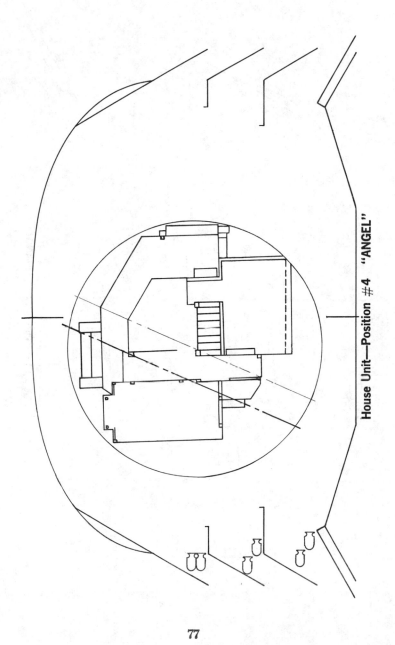

House Unit—Position #4   "ANGEL"

77

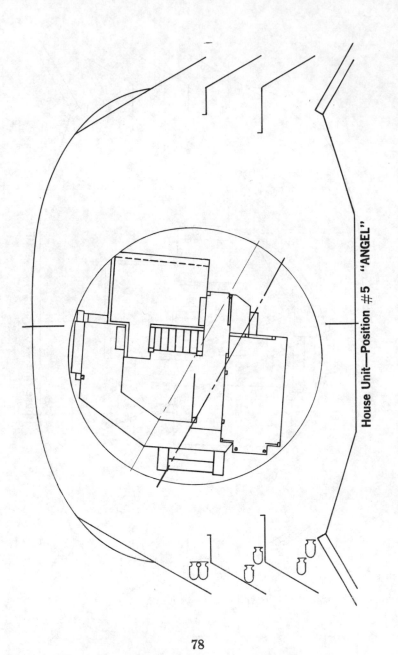

House Unit—Position #5   "ANGEL"

78

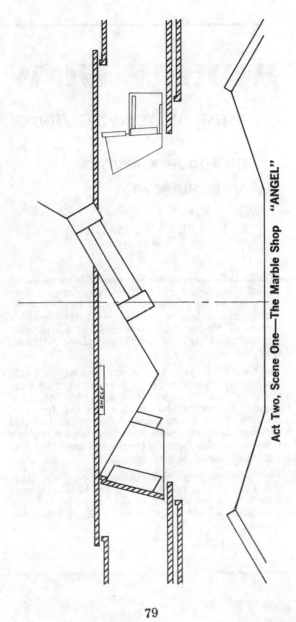

Act Two, Scene One—The Marble Shop   "ANGEL"

SHELF

HERE'S HOW

A Basic Stagecraft Book

**THOROUGHLY REVISED
AND ENLARGED**

by HERBERT V. HAKE

COVERING 59 topics on the essentials of stagecraft (13 of them brand new). *Here's How* meets a very real need in the educational theater. It gives to directors and others concerned with the technical aspects of play production a complete and graphic explanation of ways of handling fundamental stagecraft problems.

The book is exceptional on several counts. It not only treats every topic thoroughly, but does so in an easy-to-read style every layman can understand. Most important, it is prepared in such a way that for every topic there is a facing page of illustrations (original drawings and photographs)—thus giving the reader a complete graphic presentation of the topic along with the textual description of the topic.

Because of the large type, the large size of the pages (9" x 12"), and the flexible metal binding, *Here's How* will lie flat when opened and can be laid on a workbench for a director to read while in a *standing* position.

#104